Darius

sink or swim
MY STORY

headline

First published in 2003
by HEADLINE BOOK PUBLISHING

10 9 8 7 6 5 4 3 2

Every effort has been made to fulfil requirements
with regard to reproducing copyright material.
The author and publisher will be glad to rectify
any omissions at the earliest opportunity.

Cataloguing in Publication Data is available from
the British Library

Designed by Perfect Bound Ltd
Photography by Bright Masih © 19 Merchandising
Ltd, except page 52 Granada, page 151 Richard
Young/Rex Features and page 178 Katrina Aldous.
Colour reproduction by Spectrum Colour
Printed and bound in France by Pollina, L90905

ISBN 0 7553 1281 3

HEADLINE BOOK PUBLISHING
A division of Hodder Headline
338 Euston Road
London NW1 3BH

www.headline.co.uk

For my dear father,
I hope you find your beach…

Contents

chapter one

rushes

Pitch black. Heart pounding. This is it. I am standing in the dark, waiting. I've been waiting for this moment for as long as I can remember – the beginning of my first tour. Backstage, my guitar slung over my shoulder, I stand face to face with the chance to do what I've always wanted to do, the chance to prove so many people wrong. I got knocked down, but I got back up. And now I'm doing what I believe in. My nerves are jangling. Adrenaline rushes through me. I feel like I'm on the edge, ready to freefall...

I've got a theory that performers belong to the same gene pool as people who love dangerous sports.

I've got a theory that performers belong to the same gene pool as people who love dangerous sports. The risks may be different, but they say you get the same rush. There's no safety net on stage. Nobody catches you if you fall.

I felt sick with nerves before my first school gig. I was singing lead vocal in Jade, the band I formed when I was sixteen during the height of Britpop and sixties nostalgia. It was an inspiring period for a teenage musician who'd grown up listening to his mum's record collection, crammed with classics, from the Beatles to the Beach Boys, Stevie Wonder to Simon and Garfunkel.

Jade came together after I put an ad in the local Glasgow paper and met as many musicians as I could. We were a school rock band, rebels without a cause, and I wrote the songs. They weren't much good but it didn't matter. We were just very excited.

Our first gig was held in my school auditorium. It was electric. At the time, Jade's debut concert was more important than anything else, from exams to a longed-for date with the girl I fancied from another school. It summed up everything I had ever dreamed of. Standing backstage as the band began their intro was like looking over a cliff edge, about to take a bungee jump, or staring far below at the cold, hard earth seconds before I skydived out of a plane. Would I make it? I took several deep breaths and reassured myself. 'You can do it!' I whispered. 'Let's go!'

When I got on stage I was in my element. I found I could communicate more through songs and singing than I could by talking. Although I didn't have the courage to tell this beautiful girl how much I liked her – in fact her presence usually left me tongue-tied – I could say it in a song. She was out there in the audience and even if I didn't actually say her name out loud, I hoped that she realised I was singing to her and about her, in front of everybody.

This gig was also a chance to prove myself to the people who had bullied me at school. *I don't care who you are, who you think you are or who you think I am, this is what I'm about. This is who I am. You can't touch me when I'm on stage.* After the second number, a group of them started booing and heckling. So I turned the amp up high and blasted out 'Place Your Hands' by Reef, completely drowning them out. It was a great feeling. Yet after

I don't care who you are, who you think you are or who you think I am, this is what I'm about. This is who I am. You can't touch me when I'm on stage.

a while I found that the most powerful moments of the gig were when I sang quietly or whispered. The rock songs kicked the crowd up, and I loved watching people lose themselves in the music. But it was most striking when I sang an acoustic number, accompanied only by my guitar, as a single light lit the stage.

One of our favourites was a ballad. I wanted to create an intimacy between the audience and myself, like I was singing a love song to the girl I was mad about, one on one. I imagined the scenario: the two of us alone in her bedroom, sitting on a small sofa. Suddenly I had a flash of inspiration. Earlier on I had seen a couch backstage that had been used in one of the school plays, so I walked into the wings and dragged it right to the front of the stage, further forward than the monitors. I sat cross-legged, picked up my guitar and began to sing. Within seconds there was a hushed silence throughout the hall. It felt amazing to be able to create such an atmosphere.

I was flying on a high when the gig came to an end. The feelings I'd had on stage confirmed for me once and for all that my destiny lay in writing and performing music. I'd known from the age of four that I wanted to be a singer, but it was very hard to get people to take me seriously when I told them about my dreams.

They would ask me what I wanted to do when I grew up and I'd say, 'I want to be a singer.'

'What do you think you'll do if you're not a singer?' was the standard reply. It was so frustrating.

From the age of thirteen, when I learnt to play the guitar, if they asked the same question, I'd say, 'I'm going to write songs and be a singer.' It was no longer, 'I *want* to be.' It was, 'I'm *going* to be.'

'But realistically, if that doesn't work out, what's your back-up plan?' they'd always say.

'I don't have a back-up plan.' I'd say. 'I've only got one parachute.'

I was very lucky to go to a good school – my parents had put aside money for me to go to the Glasgow Academy – and my first two years there were fantastic. I was passionate about music and drama, and loved sports, but my

I was on such a high when the gig came to an end. The feelings I'd had on stage confirmed for me once and for all that my destiny lay in writing and performing music.

I was never really accepted by the sportsmen because I was getting 'A's in class. It was an isolating experience.

parents encouraged me to stay focused academically. It was at school that I developed my motto 'work hard, play hard'. But things changed when they closed the drama department and, as a result, the music department shrank. Suddenly I had no creative outlet, no way to truly express myself artistically.

Before that I'd performed in a couple of school productions. I was the bloodthirsty Transylvanian in *Dracula*, and then my love of musicals was sparked by *West Side Story* and *Joseph and the Amazing Technicolor Dreamcoat*. The next year I picked a pocket or two playing Fagin in *Oliver!*

After the drama department closed, I tried to get plays up and running with help from some of the teachers. I think I caused some friction between myself and one teacher who wanted to put on a production of *The Mikado*. She started holding auditions, but when I heard about it I suggested to the other students that it wasn't such a good idea. 'Come on! We should be doing something like *Grease*, not some stuffy production like *The Mikado*.' Unfortunately this got me a bit of a reputation for being a rebel among the teachers. As a result, neither of the shows got off the ground. I realised for the first time that sometimes being strong-minded can land you in deep water.

To make things worse, I didn't fit in with the rest of my class. I had a couple of really good girl friends, but the guys seemed to be divided into groups, none of which I really fitted into. I studied hard and so achieved good grades, but the academic kids resented me because I was good at sport. Initially I was chosen for the rugby first team because I was tall, but I secured my place through hard work. I was never really accepted by the sportsmen because I was getting 'A's in class. It was an isolating experience.

So it got to the point where I wasn't particularly liked by some of the teachers, who thought I was a rebel, the sporty kids saw the whole music thing as a bit lame, and the clever kids couldn't understand why I bothered with rugby. And the girls… Well, I fell flat on my face with girls most of the time. I was quite shy, mainly because I was afraid that if I showed how passionate I was about a girl to her face it would frighten her off. My feelings sometimes ran so deep that they scared me. I felt I was too young to be

having these kinds of powerful emotions and that I should be far more carefree and easygoing when it came to girls.

From the moment I learned to play the guitar, I found that it was much easier to express myself in words and music. When I was thirteen I wrote a love song that completely overwhelmed the girl I had written it for. At the end of the song she leaned forward with tears in her eyes and kissed me. Her reaction blew my mind. I didn't really fancy any of the girls at my school, though. Some of them were immature and the others were so taken by the sporty guys that they didn't have any time for me.

Emotional and physical bullying was a problem for me at school. Things went from bad to worse the day I stepped in to help a guy in the year below who was getting hassle from a group of older boys. Suddenly it all just turned on me. I didn't realise I was waving a red cape at a herd of bulls. I couldn't believe it. A couple of weeks earlier I'd injured my shoulder playing rugby. My arm was in sling but that didn't stop them from beating me up. I was out-numbered and I remember thinking, How can I defend myself? I stood my ground for as long as I could but I hated the sense of helplessness, of being pinned down and unable to do anything about it. After the first shock of pain was over and numbness had set in, I began to feel like a spectator to what was happening, almost like watching the action in a movie. There is a scene in *Lock, Stock and Two Smoking Barrels* – the one where Vinnie Jones is slamming the guy's head in a car door and the camera sees everything from the guy's point of view – well, I cannot watch that scene. The first time I saw it I broke down.

One day four guys followed me home. It felt like I was being cornered by a pack of wolves. They seemed to have their own code and language and they were shouting, joking, swearing and making snide comments. I tried to ignore them but then suddenly one of them stepped up very fast behind me and tapped me on the shoulder. I turned round. There was a sharp, searing pain in my face. He had head-butted me. Two of them brought me down, one on each arm. I looked up to see a foot kick down, and the sky turned black. It was horrible. I felt all the more inadequate because I was less than

From the moment I learned to play the guitar, I found that it was much easier to express myself in words and music.

fifty yards from home – and your home is supposed to be your sanctuary. If I'd shouted out, someone would probably have come to my aid, but I didn't want anyone to know about it. I didn't want anyone to know that I was numb, that the blows stopped hurting. What hurt was the boy who spat on me as the others walked away.

When I had cleaned myself up, I went home, Mum was horrified by the sight of blood and bruises. 'It was rugby,' I said, unable to look her in the eye. She knew I was hiding the truth, but I just couldn't open up to her about it. I didn't want anyone to fight my battles for me. As it happened, one of the neighbours had seen it all and called the police. When the police interviewed me, I said that I didn't know who my attackers were. At the time it made sense not to cause a fuss, but afterwards eggs were thrown at our front door, the tyres on Mum and Dad's cars were let down and the walls of our house were covered in graffiti.

The bullying went on for quite a while. I've since realised that it's often people who stand out that get bullied. I was very passionate about anything that interested me and that caught people off guard. There were other things that set me apart, too. When I was eleven I was chosen to appear in Scottish Opera productions including *Carmen*, which meant that I took time out from school to tour and appear on the Covent Garden stage in London. Later on I was singled out to apply to Oxford because of my good grades. And I was taller than most people, which in fact made being bullied all the more humiliating. I was not your obvious victim but I was still picked on.

Another reason I stood out was because my father was Persian. There were always troubles in the Middle East – like the Iran–Iraq war and then the Gulf war – and so I was called all sorts of cruel things. When I started growing facial hair above my lip, the older kids started calling me 'Saddam', unaware that my own family had had unhappy times and suffered as a result of the regime while my grandfather was an Iranian diplomat living in Baghdad. I find it very sad when I encounter prejudice, but I didn't let it get to me because I am extremely proud of my roots and rich cultural heritage. And strangely, the hostility I encountered at school set me up in a way. I really believe that what doesn't kill you makes you stronger.

It made a huge difference that I came from a happy home. I've always been very close to my family. My mother is the most graceful, calming woman I've ever met. My brother Aria is my lifelong best friend. Cyrus, the youngest of the Danesh clan, is perhaps the most insightful and inspiring person in my life. And my dad is not only a brilliant father, but also an incredible mentor and adviser. Over the years he has taught me many things.

One story he often reminds me of is from my childhood. A visit to Paris brought my parents and their three-month-old son to Notre Dame cathedral. The flickering of the prayer candles enchanted me and I wanted to touch. I was mesmerised by the beauty of the flames but didn't understand the danger of fire. Despite my father's warnings I kept reaching out. It appeared to be something wonderful. But I soon learned that it hurt like hell! To this day my dad reminds me: Not everything is as it appears to be. His words have echoed back to me again and again, with deeper meaning and resonance every time. I have learned that the gap between appearance and reality can be surprisingly wide, to say nothing of the gap between appearance and reality TV! It is a lesson I am still learning.

I found the best way to deal with the bad times at school was to get on with my own life and the things I loved best, which is why I formed Jade. The plan was to do a tour of Scotland and things were looking good after the first gig — we had gone down a storm. But as we sat and drank beer afterwards, revelling in the success of the night, my guitarist looked up and said, 'I've got something to tell you…'

By the look on his face I could tell that it was something bad. I dreaded what he was going to say next.

'I didn't tell you that I'd sat exams for the RAF,' he explained. 'Well, I got the letter today. I passed. I'm going to become a pilot.'

My heart sank. That's not what happens, I thought. That's so NOT rock and roll! Everything had gone so well up until that point. But without a guitarist the band couldn't go on. So we split.

My final school year was all about exams and university applications, although I still found time to write songs whenever

I had a spare moment – on the bus, during lunch breaks and last thing at night. I also started going out with my first serious girlfriend. I had met her on a family trip to Spain and, although she lived in London, I was determined to go on seeing her after the holiday. I used to work weekends and after school so that I could fly down on a budget airline every second weekend. I did everything – from washing cars and cleaning pizza ovens to silver service at a top restaurant. Oven-cleaning was the worst because the protective gloves they handed out were too small for me. My left hand was constantly rough from playing the guitar and then my right hand became calloused from all that scrubbing. Still, I thought I was being very grown up, jetting off to see my girlfriend in another city. I was in love with the idea of being in love – being practical didn't come into it.

My emotional world revolved around this girl. She was my first love and I really fell for her. But one Friday night, just before I jumped on my flight to see her, she tried to call things off. 'I can't go on like this,' she said. 'I want to see you every day, not just every second weekend.'

'What about every weekend?' I suggested. 'You could fly up and see me.'

A pause. An excuse. There was definitely something wrong.

It was the Easter holidays and another friend I'd met on holiday in Spain had organised a house party. I arrived late. My girlfriend was there. She was cold with me and just wouldn't give me any answers. I was frantic inside, although I tried to keep cool. 'What's wrong? What can I do to make it right?' I kept asking.

'It's me, it's me,' she said.

'Look, sort yourself out and communicate with me,' I said angrily and stormed off.

'Do you know anything about this?' I asked my friend. He wasn't saying a lot either, so I had a drink with the boys and tried in vain to enjoy the party for a couple hours. I needed to speak to her and find out what was really on her mind but I couldn't find my girlfriend anywhere. The music was loud, people were dancing, joking and filtering in and out of different

The gap between appearance and reality can be surprisingly wide, to say nothing of the gap between appearance and reality TV!

rooms. Then I walked into my friend's room. I froze. The two of them were together on the bed. What do you do in a situation like that? What do you say? It felt like the bottom had fallen out of my world. I wanted to be sick.

I felt a deep sense of betrayal. In the weeks that followed she sent me pleading letters and, although I forgave her, I told her I didn't want her in my life anymore. Being cheated on had outlined the dos and don'ts of a relationship very clearly for me. It defined the set of rules by which I conduct myself in relationships. From that point onwards, I was reminded that you should always treat others as you would like to be treated. Unfortunately I learned it the hard way, but it's a lesson I'll never forget.

Back at home, my parents had always hoped I would go to Oxford University and study sciences, but after Mum had my little brother Cyrus, I

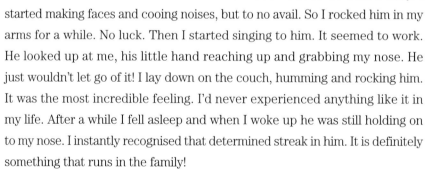

decided that I wanted to be nearer home and be the big brother to the most incredible little man in my life.

I will never forget the night Mum brought him home from hospital. She was exhausted after a long labour. She handed Cyrus to me and lay down to rest for a few minutes. Not surprisingly, she passed out the moment her head hit the pillow. But Cyrus was wide awake, full of beans, gurgling away. Then he started crying. I looked at his tiny, dimpled face and realised that I didn't have a clue what to do with a baby. I started making faces and cooing noises, but to no avail. So I rocked him in my arms for a while. No luck. Then I started singing to him. It seemed to work. He looked up at me, his little hand reaching up and grabbing my nose. He just wouldn't let go of it! I lay down on the couch, humming and rocking him. It was the most incredible feeling. I'd never experienced anything like it in my life. After a while I fell asleep and when I woke up he was still holding on to my nose. I instantly recognised that determined streak in him. It is definitely something that runs in the family!

I decided that I wanted to experience the independence of moving away from home, so I didn't want to study in Glasgow, but still wanted to be near enough that Cyrus would grow up knowing his older brother. Against my parents' preference, I thought it would be a good idea to take an arts subject like English literature. Immersing myself in words and literature would help me to become a better lyricist and it would mean having enough spare time to

To write good songs you need to be able to tell stories, and good stories come from life experience. It was time for late nights and lie-ins, dates with girls and wild parties with friends…

improve my songwriting. Most importantly perhaps, to write good songs you need to be able to tell stories, and good stories come from life experience. It was time for late nights and lie-ins, dates with girls and wild parties with friends – and all while trying to keep Mum and Dad happy of course. So I packed my bags and headed to Edinburgh University. The plan was to build a home studio and record the songs I'd written so that I could leave university with a degree under my belt, demo in hand, hungry for a major record deal. It was hard disappointing my parents' hopes, but it motivated me. I had to succeed at my own goals and make them proud.

It seemed like the right decision. University was a fresh start and new beginning – I was far happier than I had been at school. In the first week I met my two best friends, Sean and Simon. I helped them set up Edinburgh's premier student production company within six months. We organised and produced all kinds of events, from the biggest student production of *Grease,*  to the most notorious club nights – flying the best DJs up from London, scouting the sexiest dancers and making sure the drinks were cheap. They called us the Three Musketeers – 'All for one and one for all…'. We were young and enjoying ourselves. Word spread and we got a bit of a reputation. At one club night there was a queue of students in the street an hour before the venue had even opened. We made a stack of cash and lost a bundle, but it balanced out in the end.

I continued writing songs at university. I turned up at an open-mike night at the Tron pub in Edinburgh a couple of times and performed an acoustic set on my guitar. Sean and Simon came to watch me play as I have always relied on them to give me their honest opinions. Some songs were good, some were bad, a few were downright awful. One Monday Johnnie, my good friend from Glasgow, came along to watch. 'Darius, someone should give you a record deal,' he said afterwards. (I think he'd had quite a few pints.) It was the best compliment anyone could ever have given me. Well, that's what friends are for, isn't it?

By the time I was at university, Johnnie had decided that he wanted to be a TV producer. So when he told me that he was auditioning to be a TV presenter, I was slightly confused. But I didn't question it, I just went along to encourage him. Or that was the plan, anyway.

I'd been out to a big Latino party in Glasgow the night before and had got home at sunrise. 11.30a.m. – I awoke to a phone call from Johnnie, who asked if I wanted to meet him for lunch. 'But you'll have to hurry,' he said. 'I've been recalled to an audition at 2p.m., so I haven't got much time.' I jumped out of bed, still wearing my clothes from the night before, and was out of the house within five minutes – without bothering to change out of my tight black trousers and ghastly black satin Latino shirt with its big collar.

After lunch Johnnie said, 'I'd better get back now. Do you want to come?' I wanted to support him, so I went along. When we got to the studios, he disappeared into another part of the building and I was supposed to sit in the 'family area'. But I couldn't cheer him on if I waited there, could I? So I decided to try and blag my way into the audition room.

'What are you here for?' asked the producer.

I wasn't going to get anywhere unless I had a good excuse, so I said the first thing that came into my head.

'Well I'm here to audition but I was late…because I came from Glasgow and…ah, yes, I had a car crash.'

'You're full of shit,' she laughed.

'I'm not,' I protested. 'I'm just recovering from last night…because it was, er, my friend's twenty-first.' More childish chat.

For some reason she seemed to warm to me. 'I'd like to audition for you,' I said, sensing the thaw.

'No,' she said firmly.

'Why not?' I asked.

'I don't have time. Anyway, we're doing the recalls now.'

Minutes later I saw her eating a sandwich in the canteen. I decided to push my luck, so I bee-lined her and said cheekily, 'Let me audition for you while you have lunch. If not, at least let me entertain you.'

'Go on then,' she sighed.

'What do you want me to do?' I asked.

'Present the weather,' she said.

Well, I was wearing an awful black satin shirt and so I decided to do a bit of role-play. Just for a laugh I started speaking in an exaggerated Spanish accent. 'Laydeez and gentlemen, welcome to the weather show. My name is Pedro, your only Latin-lover weatherman. Laydeez grab your brolleez,

My immediate reaction was to think, What?! I've got it? But I don't actually want to be a weatherman!

you're going to get wet. In the south-east a stormy front eez coming like tigers making love in ze clouds.'

The producer started laughing. 'You're through,' she said.

I didn't take any of it seriously. I hadn't been around for the first set of auditions and anyway, I was there for Johnnie. When I was interviewed by one of the producers and asked what my ambitions were, I simply told the truth and said that I was a singer-songwriter with plans to release my music when I finished university. I was joking around with Johnnie when someone approached us and said we had *both* got through to the penultimate round of the auditions. We thought it was hilarious.

Later they started calling out the names of the final five. Four names down and I was waiting for them to call Johnnie's name – but instead they called out *mine*. I was gutted. This was for him, not for me. I'd just come to support him. I felt so guilty. Fortunately Johnnie thought it was funny. In fact from that moment on, we became better friends.

While we were waiting for the final result to be announced, I got talking to one of the judges. After chatting away for a while, he whispered, 'By the way, I'm not supposed to tell you this, but you've got the job.'

My immediate reaction was to think, What?! I've got it? But I don't actually want to be a weatherman!

The producer of the show came back into the room and called us together. Then he announced the winner – and said someone else's name. Well, I was actually quite relieved. The other judge apologised for raising my hopes, I told him I wasn't bothered at all. It turned out that the producer had said at the final moment, 'Look, this guy doesn't want to be a weatherman. He wants to be a singer.' Of course I did. I had talked my way out of the job. Phew!

I wasn't any nearer to achieving my dreams, but it had been a great ride and I was up for any twist or turn. I was optimistic, energetic, bursting with naïve enthusiasm. Life stretched before me like a vast, glittering ocean. As I stood on the shore, little did I know that the wind was picking up and somewhere in the distance, a storm was brewing…

dive in

As I start singing the Britney Spears song, 'Baby One More Time', it strikes me that I have really no idea why I'm here or what I'm doing. Halfway through the song, Nicki Chapman interrupts.

'Enough, thank you. I find your version of this song offensive.'

That's it. My big audition is at an end and I've messed it up. As I realise what I've done, all I can think is, Why didn't I take it more seriously?

11a.m. on 3 September 2000, Glasgow, Scotland. The last twenty-four hours had been a bit of a blur. How had I got here? What had I just done? Well, it had all started the morning before, with an early phone call from Johnnie.

It was 7a.m. to be precise. Johnnie was already up, helping out with his dad's landscaping business. I, on the other hand, was fast asleep on the downstairs pull-out bed at my parents' house, still wearing my clothes from the night before (again!). I'd been out very late and hadn't wanted to disturb anyone when I came in.

The ring tone of my mobile cut through my deep unconsciousness. I reached for the phone and picked up the call automatically, without really registering what I was doing. The voice on the other end sounded excited.

'Darius, there's an audition on the radio! And if you win, you get a record deal!'

I hardly heard what he said. Sleep was weighing down my eyelids, refusing to let them open.

'Johnnie, I'll call you later,' was all I managed to say before I dropped the phone and slipped back into dreaming.

A minute later the phone rang again.

'Darius, wake up!' shouted Johnnie. 'You've got to call Beat 106FM and sing down the phone to them. If you don't do it now, you'll lose your chance of a record deal.' He sounded frantic.

But sleep wouldn't let me go. 'Mmmmm…I'll talk to you later,' I murmured, and again the phone dropped out of my hand.

He rang again, I hung up again. He called me for the fourth time.

'Darius, if you don't ring the radio station right now, I'm calling for you.'

If he was trying to threaten me into action, it wasn't working. 'Are you trying to torture me or something?' I laughed sleepily. 'I'm not doing any audition today. I'll call you later.' And I hung up.

The land line rang and rang. I didn't answer. A moment later Mum passed through the hall on her way out to work. 'Darius!' she called. 'There's a radio station on the phone. They want to speak to you.'

All I wanted was sleep, more sleep, please.

'Darius, answer the phone! I'm leaving right now.'

She left, leaving the phone off the hook and the radio station hanging on the line.

There was nothing else for it. I had to wake up. I stumbled to the phone and put it to my ear.

'Hello,' I growled. I had a bad case of 'morning voice'.

'Is this Darius Danesh?'

'Yes.'

'So what are you going to sing for us?'

What? I thought. Clouds of sleep were still drifting through my head, fogging up my brain. 'Erm, I don't know what I'm going to sing for you,' I replied hazily.

'Is this a wind-up?' asked the voice on the other end. 'We were told to call this number because you were trying to get through to us.'

Suddenly I woke up and realised what was happening.

'We'll call you back in five minutes and you'll be live on air. You've got to sing a well-known song, OK?'

I got a call from the radio station. 'You've won your way through to our final audition tomorrow morning. Can you come and sing live in a studio?'

They hung up.

Instantly I dialled Johnnie's number. 'What do you think you're doing?' I shouted. 'You gave them my name and my number and now I've got to sing a song down the phone!'

I switched on the radio and tuned it to Beat 106FM. 'And up next we've got Darius, Jon and Vanessa in our talent search competition,' said the announcer.

I thought, So I'm supposed to sing over the telephone line and from that they can judge whether I'm a good singer? And then they're going to give me a record deal if I win? It didn't make sense.

'You wake me up for this?' I asked Johnnie, who was still on the line. 'I mean, at least ring me up when there's another weatherman competition!'

And I slammed the phone down. Right, I thought. I'm going to get him back for this. So I sat down and started scribbling some lyrics on a piece of paper. I can't remember exactly what I wrote, but it was basically a rude version of 'Baby One More Time' by Britney Spears, full of silly rhymes and swear words. It was deliberately bad and I assumed that I'd be bleeped out and cut off the moment I started singing, but I didn't care. I just wanted to have a dig at Johnnie.

The radio station called back and I sang the song over the phone. When I'd finished there was a pause at the end of the line and I thought, Well, they've obviously bleeped me out. But then the DJ said, 'Darius, we had to cut the end of that song off, but thanks for calling and good luck.' That was that, or so I thought. I had no idea that my 'performance' instantly prompted a burst of calls from listeners asking, 'Who was that? He was wicked!' Which explains why, a few hours later, I got a call from the radio station. 'You've won your way through to our final audition tomorrow morning. Can you come and sing live in a studio?'

This is definitely a wind-up, I thought. I phoned Johnnie. 'Did you get your dad or one of your friends to phone me up and say that I was through to the next round of the competition?' I asked accusingly.

'No, mate,' he replied, genuinely surprised. 'It must be true.'

The next morning Johnnie and his girlfriend picked me up at 7.30a.m. and took me to the Scottish TV studios in Glasgow. I took my guitar along and sang the same version of 'Baby One More Time', with the rewritten lyrics. It was all a big joke. Then someone told me that I'd won. But I can't have won a record deal! I thought. What is this all about?

The audition was being aired live on the radio and suddenly there was a drum roll. 'Congratulations Darius,' said the presenter, 'You've won. How do you feel?'

'Great!' I replied, not knowing at all how I 'felt'. I didn't know what to say. I just wanted to find out what I'd got myself into. 'What exactly does this mean? Have I got a slot on Beat 106 singing jingles?' I joked.

'No,' laughed the presenter. 'We're now whisking you away to meet a group of television producers at the next round of the auditions.'

'What?' At this point I was feeling very confused. It was a bit like watching a movie that starts bang in the middle of the action. All you can do is try to figure out who the people are, what the relationships are between them and why you're watching them – until the major plot lines kick in. And in this case it definitely took a while to catch up with the bigger picture. Because the next minute I was in a car with a journalist holding a microphone to my face and firing questions at me. We drew up outside a warehouse building where I saw literally hundreds of kids queuing up, waiting expectantly. I'd never come across anything quite like it before.

*In front of
me were three
people –
two men and
a woman –
sitting
behind a
desk, with
cameras
trained on
them. It all
seemed very
small scale*

We got out of the car and the radio crew took me straight to the front of the queue. What do I do now? I wondered. The journalist started interviewing people in the line and then turned to me. 'And how do you feel now, Darius?'

I decided to try the direct approach. 'Look, I don't know what the hell's happening! What is this?'

Meanwhile, I'd missed the introductory talk and things were moving fast. I was second in the queue; in front of me was a pretty Scottish girl who smiled at me. Before I had a chance to ask her what it was all about, I was directed into a room and told to sing.

I looked around the room. In front of me were three people – two men and a woman – sitting behind a desk, with cameras trained on them. It all seemed very small scale, so I thought to myself, OK, they're making a documentary about the radio programme. Still, there wasn't really time to think, so I picked up my guitar and started singing 'Baby One More Time', the rude version.

'Could you sing without the guitar, please?' asked one of the people behind the desk.

Now I was really confused. I wanted to play my guitar. But I put it down, as requested, and started singing unaccompanied. Just as I got to a particularly rude bit in the chorus, the female judge interrupted.

'Enough, thank you. I find your version of this song offensive.'

I stopped singing, cut short, and realised that I'd put my foot in it. The next person entered the room to sing and I had no choice but to leave. I walked out and bumped into the radio crew. It turned out that they hadn't been allowed to record my performance.

Hold on a minute, I thought. This thing is obviously much bigger than Beat 106 if they don't even have access to the audition room. It wasn't until afterwards that I figured out that the radio station were piggy-backing off the filming to entertain their listeners, holding their own auditions on air just as a gimmick. As it happened, I could have just turned up to the audition without singing on the radio at all. But I guess at least it got me to the front of the queue.

Then it hit me. This was a serious audition and I'd messed up already. It was a horrible moment.

I started talking to some of the other contestants and they told me about friends who were going to the London auditions. That meant that this was a nationwide event, which put a completely different perspective on it. So then it hit me. This was a serious audition and I'd messed up already. It was a horrible moment. I realised that I could have turned up to this audition, taken it seriously and done something with it, instead of playing the whole thing like a big joke.

One of the judges, who introduced himself as Nigel Lythgoe, sat us all down and started taking us through the audition. And as he was talking it became clear that this was an audition for a pop group, not a solo artist. The information was seeping out to me in small measures and I was trying to piece it all together. So it's for a pop group. But hold on, I don't actually want to be in a pop group...

It reminded me of the time when I thought, But wait a minute, I don't want to be a weatherman! And it was at that moment that I decided to walk out and forget about the whole thing. It was obvious that I hadn't got through the audition and I didn't want to be in a pop group anyway. But as I picked up my guitar, I took a last look around the room. I hadn't had the chance to play it, I hadn't shown them what I could do. From the main audition room I could hear another boy singing Robbie Williams' 'Angels'. It made me smile to think what Robbie had achieved and where he'd come from. From manufactured boy band to credible solo artist, he'd done it. Who was to say it couldn't be done again? Did Robbie know who he'd become when he was in Take That? If I won a place in this pop group could I use it as a stepping-stone to releasing my own music one day? I thought to myself you'll never know unless you try. I can't let this moment pass me by. I had to dive in.

So I returned to the audition room and made my apologies. 'I'm really sorry,' I said. 'I've just come from this radio audition where they encouraged me to sing that version of the song. I had no idea what the situation was here. Can you give me another chance?'

The answer was yes.

'Is it all right if I sing a different song?' I asked.

There was a pause. 'No, sing the Britney song again,' said the female judge, whose name, I soon found out, was Nicki Chapman. She had co-managed Billie Piper and had a key role in promotions for Take That and the Spice Girls.

I think Nicki enjoyed the fact that I was singing a girl's song. I sang the song straight and was immediately told that I'd got through to the next round of auditions. Now it was time to find out what this was all about. All I needed to do was talk to someone who would give me a few straight answers. Little did I know that so many of my questions would go unanswered, or that it would be more than six months before I had any real idea of what I had got myself into.

The callbacks were held at the National Indoor Arena in Birmingham a few weeks later. When I arrived at the hotel that we had been booked into, the other contestants were in a frenzy of worry about which room they would get and who they were neighbours with. I sat in the lobby thinking, This feels like a school trip! I just wanted to focus on doing well the  next day so I collected my keys and retreated to my room for some head space.

I reasoned with myself that I could only get on in this competition if I could convince the judges that I wanted to be in a pop group, even though that was not my ambition. But it wouldn't be the end of the world if I got into this band. I knew where I wanted to go, I just didn't know how to get there. Perhaps this was as good a way as any. What the hell, I was going to give it a go. What's more, the judges had said that they were looking to form a boy/girl equivalent of All Saints. Pop groups surely don't come any cooler.

Once I'd decided that this was something I wanted to succeed at, I just went for it, tackling every obstacle that presented itself. There was a real competitive edge to it, because I hate losing, and the knock-on effect of taking things more seriously was that I started to care far more about the outcome. By the end I cared too much. That was my mistake. I went from just having fun to really worrying about what the judges were looking for and trying too hard. Worse still, I was trying too hard to be something I wasn't.

One of the incentives for getting into the band was that we would apparently have a chance to work with the best producers in the business.

Once I'd decided that this was something I wanted to succeed at, I just went for it, tackling every obstacle that presented itself.

There was also a lot of talk among the contestants about the money that would be made, the flash cars, cool pads and exotic holidays that wealth would bring us. It was difficult not to be affected by those kinds of images. They definitely turned my head at first glance.

I don't think the judges realised that I had never been to a music audition before. Some of the other contestants thought that I had been to stage school or was already a professional singer. Girls were coming up to me asking for advice while I stood there thinking, Why are you asking me? I haven't got a clue!

There I was, among stage-school graduates and semi-professional singers – people who were trained – and I hadn't had any form of training at all. One school gig and some classical singing didn't count as pop experience. Looking back on the person I was then, at nineteen, I realise now that I was naïve and insecure. I was still in the throes of working out who I was and I wanted instant answers. The lifebuoy that kept me afloat was my passion for music. I had nothing else, no experience of being in a real band, gigging, or even karaoke. I came across as confident, energetic, enthusiastic and passionate about everything. I think that's the essence of me. So that's the way I appeared. But I was feeling very vulnerable at the time. Once more it was the appearance-and-reality lesson that my dad had told me about. I tried to overcompensate for my sense of inadequacy and as time went on I began to behave out of character. What people saw, wasn't how I felt. There were rip currents beneath the calm water's surface.

During the Birmingham callbacks the judges reduced the number of contestants from 168 to thirty-three. Before each round we were told exactly what to sing. I think this was quite a good thing because although I had strong ideas about what I thought I wanted to do, I had to conform if I was going to get anywhere.

One morning Nigel Lythgoe gathered us together and explained, 'This band is all about chemistry, so next we're going to do a series of duets.'

I began trying to predict what it was they wanted. Instead of relying on my gut reaction, I tried to second-guess them the whole time. It was something I regretted later.

My partner and I were given the Elton John and Kiki Dee song, 'Don't Go Breaking My Heart'. We were about fourth or fifth in line to perform it. I noticed that the couples that went before us didn't really treat their songs as duets and there was very little interaction between them. They weren't particularly singing to each other, they were each singing to the camera, trying to make an individual impression.

When it came to our turn, the image of Olivia Newton-John and John Travolta's 'You're the One that I Want' in *Grease* flashed into my mind. So as we sang, I grabbed the girl's hand, span her around and looked into her eyes. It seemed the natural thing to do, although she was a bit taken aback because we hadn't rehearsed it that way. Suddenly there *was* a real chemistry there. People were cheering us on before we'd reached the end of the song. Afterwards Nigel Lythgoe stood in front of the camera and roared, 'That is what you should all be doing! It's a duet, you should be singing *to each other*. I want everyone who's had their turn to go and practise for ten minutes, then come back and do it again.'

That's when I realised that the judges might not always reveal what they were looking for – you just had to find it for yourself. Soon afterwards I began trying to predict what it was they wanted. Instead of relying on my gut reaction, I tried to second-guess them the whole time. It was something I regretted later. I hated the fact that I'd turned into a performing dog, jumping through hoops.

At another point we had to learn a dance routine with Janet Jackson's choreographers. It wasn't me, but I threw myself into it. The thought of doing a Janet Jackson dance routine seems ridiculous now, but at the time I just got on with it. I was giving my all, throwing everything at the wall to see if it would stick and how the judges would react. My mind was taken up with trying to be something that I wasn't, the person I thought that the judges wanted, even though I didn't know what they wanted.

'What are you looking for?' I kept asking.

The answer they always gave me was, 'Darius, we'll know when we find it.'

I hated the fact that I'd turned into a performing dog, jumping through hoops.

I realised that the 'X-factor' the judges were looking for was not just a combination of talent and charisma, but attitude also.

I went on pushing for answers. 'Well, what kind of group are you putting together?' I didn't give up. I had to know more. 'What's the creative direction? What's the music going to be like? Is it R&B, pop or something with a rock influence?'

They wouldn't tell me. 'None of that matters now,' they said. 'It's all about the chemistry.' I just became more and more confused.

On the upside, I soon started getting to know some of the other contestants, who turned out to be an excited and eclectic group from all walks of life. I got on very well with a guy called Raymond, who I thought was the most gifted singer of all. His voice technically blew mine out of the water, but whereas I remained positive and wanted to strive through to each new round, he didn't seem to care what happened. I realised that the 'X-factor' the judges were looking for was not just a combination of talent and charisma, but attitude also.

Then there was Taz. He called me Big D and I found myself behaving like his surrogate big brother. I was also close to Michelle, a bubbly, light-hearted club dancer who was passionate about the audition. I respected how she took important things seriously. Tony, the Irish charmer and Jessica, the sexy girl-next-door with a sultry voice, shared that same focus, and both had a sense of humour. We often enjoyed late-night drinks at the hotel bar bouncing ideas off each other about the future of pop, bonded by the desire to be creative rather than be part of something manufactured. I had a gut feeling they'd each find their own way, whatever happened. But I had no way of knowing then that with Kelli and Kevin they'd go on to become Liberty X.

Kym Marsh and I also became friends. I saw a feisty, determined streak in her that I liked. Of the five who eventually made it into the band, I got on with her the best.

Mylene was very quiet and much harder to get to know. I remember watching her at lunch one day sitting on the floor all alone. I sat down with her, smiled and tried to get to know her. But it was like hearing someone's

Nigel began calling out names, peering at us from over his glasses. Nobody was quite sure what it meant to have your name called. Did it mean you were going through to the next stage or not?

CV. Normally I can get a smile out of someone with a couple of cheeky jokes, but she wasn't biting on it.

As time went on I began to peel away at the realisation that the auditions were as much about making good TV as they were about making music. I saw Nigel Lythgoe as the puppet-master. One of the great TV producers, who had worked on everything from *An Audience With…The Spice Girls* to *Blind Date* and *Gladiators*, he knew exactly what he was doing. I didn't fully know what editing could do until months after the auditions, when the whole thing was televised, but I was catching on fast.

At the eleventh hour of the Birmingham audition they herded us into a hall and left us to wait for the news of who was going through to the London auditions. There were sixty contestants, but around half of us would be sent home. Everyone sat cross-legged on the floor, which took me back to my early school days when we would sit and listen obediently as the head called out names for detention. Nigel Lythgoe was the headmaster and we were his pupils.

Nigel began calling out names, peering at us from over his glasses. Nobody was quite sure what it meant to have your name called. Did it mean that you were going through to the next stage or not? Everyone whose name was called was asked to stand up. And there I sat, on the floor, looking at who was standing up and thinking, She's really good and I want to be in her group! I want to stand up! But then I'd think, No, that other girl standing didn't sing so well. I want to stay firmly on the ground, because that means that I'll get through. Or does it?

Like everyone else, I was questioning myself, questioning the people around me, questioning whether all this was worth it, mind in overdrive, going nuts. We were all suffering from paralysis by analysis. People were breaking down in tears even before their names were called out. The room was taut with emotion and in a funny way I was really enjoying it all. I was thinking, This is great! They've got us strung up – I've been hooked and they've drawn the line in. But at least I am aware of it.

The twenty-seven people standing up were asked to go into another room. As they started leaving I realised that, whether I was through to

> *The auditions were as much about making good TV as they were about making music. I saw Nigel Lythgoe as the puppet-master.*

It felt so wonderful to succeed in the wake of tears and drama. I was determined to get through. I just had to.

the next stage or not, I probably wouldn't see them again. We said goodbye to each other without knowing the other's fate.

At first those of us remaining sat spread out, but as the minutes ticked away we began to move closer together, like frightened cattle. It grew into the biggest group hug I've ever seen. Hands found hands, arms hooked over shoulders. It was emotional and surreal in equal measure. You didn't know who you were holding – we were all just holding each other and feeling the fraught tension. Our hopes and dreams were dangled before us, like a carrot on a stick, just out of reach.

Then, a single voice cut through. Someone started singing Bill Withers' 'Lean On Me'. Suddenly, from something artificial and orchestrated, came something organic. We all started singing along. We hadn't sung as a group before, but as we started to improvise harmonies and counter-melodies, the rendition of that song turned into something that was far stronger, far deeper, than any individual audition. Our hopes and our voices resounded in the room.

Nigel Lythgoe returned. 'I'm sorry, I've got bad news,' he said. At this point anyone who was holding back tears just started crying. 'Your friends next door didn't get in,' he continued. 'You've made it through to London.'

Suddenly, release. A rush of emotion as everyone screamed and jumped up in a surge of hysteria. Shouts, laughter, whoops of joy. Finally cut free from tension, I threw someone over my shoulder and ran around like a mad man. It was an incredible feeling. That moment was a turning point for me. It was as if the judges had thrown down the gauntlet. It struck me how much I wanted to get into the band now – if only to experience that amazing high again. It felt so wonderful to succeed in the wake of tears and drama. I was determined to get through. I just had to.

chapter three

chrysalis to butterfly

I grab Noel, pull him into the kitchen and whisper,

'Congratulations.'

'What?' he asks. He hasn't a clue what I am getting at.

'You're in,' I say. 'Whatever you do, make the most of

this and enjoy every minute.'

He looks confused. He doesn't know how to take it.

'I've not got in. It could be anyone,' he protests. But I am

sure. I know.

And I'm right.

It was great to be back in London. Although the streets are not paved with gold, and it's a bustling, polluted hive, there was something exciting about trying to break into music in the capital. I didn't have a chance to get my bearings or catch up with friends and family though. My feet didn't hit the ground. The next series of callback auditions took up almost every waking moment, in the form of a five-day assault course.

At the London Weekend Television rehearsal rooms in Brixton I said to the judges, 'I'm passionate about songwriting. If I get into the band I hope my creative contributions would be thrown in the pot.' I didn't think it would do me any harm to say what I did. After all, having a songwriter in the group could only be a bonus, couldn't it? The judges kept referring to All Saints and it was well known that Shaznay wrote most of the band's music. All Saints records involved input from the artist musically, and in style and character. Take That had Gary Barlow writing the music. I couldn't help pointing that out and I wouldn't let it go.

I kept pushing. On the final day of the auditions I said, 'Will you let me sing an original song?'

They mulled over the idea, deliberated, and finally said it would be OK.

'If the song is any good or not, you will just judge me on the basis of my singing, right?'

'Of course.'

I started singing a song I'd written, a cappella.

They stopped me before I'd finished singing it. 'We don't want to judge you on the basis of that song.'

'Why?' I asked.

There was a pause. 'Because we don't think it's any good.'

This completely cut me down. It occurred to me that perhaps, no matter what I did, they'd already decided that I wasn't what they were looking for. I thought the song was OK. It was a decent pop song.

Their last comment was, 'Darius, you're not nearly as good a songwriter as you are a singer, so don't try and be something you're not.'

This infuriated me. I was spun round – and then I started doubting myself. I didn't know whether they were saying these things to wind me up, to put me down or just because they were genuinely trying to give me constructive criticism. These were seasoned professionals and I respected them for being at the top of their games within their respective industries – a director of A&R at Polydor, controller of entertainment and comedy at LWT and one of the team behind the Spice Girls promotions. Basically, they were saying that I couldn't write songs, and I faced the daunting prospect that they were right. I had a lot of rethinking to do.

They came up with a comment that they reeled off time and again: 'That song doesn't show off your full range.' If I had a pound for every time I heard them say those words, I'd be a millionaire by now, I thought.

I had a stomach bug that day. I had vomited earlier and felt light-headed for hours afterwards. On camera Nigel Lythgoe told me to pull myself together. Five minutes later, off camera, he put his hand on my shoulder and said, 'Are you all right? You know I had to be tough with you for the cameras.' So he was playing a game with me, moving effortlessly between appearance and reality.

I sensed that I wasn't going to get through to the final ten, but after watching the others audition I couldn't help wanting another shot. So I went back to the judges and said, 'Since you don't like my song, I'd like to sing you a cover, if you will allow me. Can I have a second chance?'

I was about to hit self-destruct.

I excused myself and went to the toilet, where I had some kind of Mexican face-off with myself in the mirror. I was definitely at the last-chance saloon. While I was psyching myself up to go in there and do something impressive, all kinds of thoughts swirled through my head. I felt confused. I felt angry. I figured that I'd already worked out who was going to get into the band by watching the judges' reactions. I was full of resentment and insecurity. Did the judges really mean all that criticism? Alone in the bathroom I again sang the song that I'd written. No, I thought. They're wrong. I don't care what they say. I like that song. I suspected that it wouldn't be shown on the programme though.

That's when I decided to sing the Britney song, the song that had started off this whole mad auditioning process. What's more, I was determined to do it in a way that nobody had ever heard before. Images from the Fat Boy Slim

Did the judges really mean all that criticism? Alone in the bathroom I again sang the song that I'd written. No, I thought. They're wrong. I don't care what they say. I like that song.

video for 'Praise You' flashed through my head. Spike Jonze filming a modern-dance troupe doing a ridiculous dance in a shopping centre is the last thing you would think of to accompany a dance track like 'Praise You'. Yet it was one of the best music videos of that year. 'Do something different,' I whispered to myself.

As I went on looking in the mirror, in another part of my brain the judges' voices were repeating, 'Darius, it doesn't show off your full range.' That phrase was enraging me now. I'll show you, I thought – by singing a song that does show off my full bloody range. Now no sane man who can sing bass lines would try to hit the high notes in that Britney song. Still, I decided to do exactly that. I sang the song through once, making it up as I went along. Having said that, what I sang in the bathroom wasn't anything like what the camera and millions of viewers saw or heard. It was improvisation all the way.

I tend to intellectualise a decision after I've made it – relying on my gut instinct at the time. Which is good, I think, because if we thought about everything we did before we did it, half the time we'd end up doing nothing. We'd just play it safe. But perhaps a little logical reasoning would have been appropriate at this point. Instead, I began to have flashbacks of all the different hoops the judges had made us jump through, especially the dance routine with Janet Jackson's choreographer, all shoulder moves and claps. Do you know what? I thought crossly. I'm going to do my own version of those moves while I'm singing.

The culmination of all these whirring thoughts was that I then went upstairs and did the silly Britney thing. It was almost like a kamikaze pilot who thinks, I might as well go down in flames. I still don't know exactly what I was doing and if you asked me to repeat what I did in those two or three minutes, I simply couldn't. I realised afterwards that a normal music audition was very different from the *Popstars* auditions. It was such an artificial scenario. No wonder I had combusted.

Even though it had been completely over-the-top, the other contestants congratulated me after my performance. Tony, who went on to be in Liberty X, came up and said, 'Hey, you showed them.'

I tend to intellectualise a decision after I've made it – relying on my gut instinct at the time.

Right, whatever you do, don't give them what they want. You can't break down. You can't give in at this point.

It was while we were waiting to be told who the final ten were that I grabbed Noel and let him know that I was convinced he was going to be in the band. I had watched Nigel and Nicki's reaction to him and, although he wasn't necessarily the strongest male vocalist, they obviously loved his boy-next-door look. It seemed to me that they filmed the judges' reactions to his performance in more detail than some of the others. I took that to mean that he was in. Meanwhile, I sensed that I was out. Now it was time to find out for sure.

Next to the audition rooms there was a huge dance studio, with mirrors along the walls and a wooden floor. A table for the judges to sit behind was set up at the far end of the studio, along with glaring lights and cameras. Individually, we had to walk right to the end of that room and sit down to hear the judges' verdicts. It was quite intimidating to open the door and have to adjust your eyes to the light before you could focus on the three figures in the distance. It seemed like a five-minute walk, although in reality it was maybe fifty metres. They called it 'The Green Mile'.

From what I understood, the judges gave their verdicts in a very formulaic way. They either built you up and then told you that you hadn't made it through, or criticised you for ages before announcing that you had made it. Lots of the contestants emerged from that room in floods of tears. And then it was my turn to walk 'The Green Mile' and find out what fate awaited me.

I'd just done my Britney thing and I'd adjusted to the idea that this was it for me, so as I was walking to the end of the room, I was thinking, Right, whatever you do, don't give them what they want. You can't break down. You can't give in at this point. I sat down – and whereas the others had each been in there for five minutes, I was there for twenty. They went through everything I'd done, right from my first audition, criticising me at every turn. Nicki Chapman said, 'I've worked with a band that had a rebel before, but you seem to be a rebel without a cause.'

Is this for TV or to wind me up? I wondered for the hundredth time. And then I said my piece. I really laid into them. 'You've not given us the opportunity to play an instrument, or sing anything but covers. The song I sang, according to you, was no good. Do you honestly think it wasn't good enough?' There was a pause. I tried again, this time addressing Paul Adam, a director of A&R at Polydor Records. 'Sir, do you not think it's about time that we were given an opportunity to sing original music in pop? You work for a record company. Instead of doing something tried and trusted, instead of creating another Steps, why don't you try and do something original? Why don't you let things develop more organically? I know there are other kids here who can contribute musically and do more than just provide a vocal on a song. But you're stifling any creative involvement. Why?'

Paul Adam replied hesitantly, 'Darius, I don't think you understand the nature of the auditions…' I don't think he expected anyone *to question* the nature of the auditions, let alone at this stage.

And then came the build-up. Nigel started saying, 'Darius, I think you've got the strongest male voice and you've got a lot of potential…' Nicky started complimenting me too. All the while I'm thinking, Don't let them raise you to an emotional peak just so they can drop you down. Keep a straight face. Don't smile. I knew what they were trying to do. I knew I could easily break down – as anyone would – but I held it together, just.

'You did a very strange thing today,' said Nigel, referring to the Britney performance, 'and it did rather over-egg the cake. We do not see you in this pop band; consequently we are not going to ask you back tomorrow.' Nigel certainly knew how to drive home a line for its best effect!

'If I hadn't sung that last song, would I still be in with a chance?' I asked.

'No, that last song didn't make the difference, but we do feel that it was the final nail in the coffin,' was the reply.

I took a deep breath and said, 'Thank you for this experience. It's one of the most valuable lessons I've ever had. But I think you're wrong. It's my dream to have a number-one

'Life is not just one opportunity. There are opportunities around us every day and all you have to do is see them. And seize them!' People often say, you've only got one shot, but you don't.

single as a solo artist and a platinum album by the time I'm thirty-five.'

I felt a surge of determination run through me. I was going to prove them wrong. I said, 'I will succeed. I don't know how, but I will succeed.' I stood up and walked out.

The tension was unbearable. I had no idea if there was going to be another camera waiting behind the next door. I kept reminding myself of my father's words, 'Life is not just one opportunity. There are opportunities around us every day and all you have to do is see them. And seize them!' People often say, you've only got one shot, but you don't. This is just another day, I told myself. It's not the end, it's just the beginning. I'll go to sleep and tomorrow will be a brand new day. There was no need to shed a tear, there was nothing to fear. I was so excited.

As it turned out, there wasn't a camera on the other side of the door. Lucky for me. The adrenaline hit my stomach and I was sick in the toilets. After splashing my face with water, I pulled my thoughts together, looked at myself in the mirror and realised how lucky I was to feel so invigorated. My thoughts drifted to my new friends who had been struck by disappointment. I found them in a room next door. 'Guys, I've had the most incredible time and I've met some fantastic people and I hope we all stay in touch.' Everyone turned and looked at me. Then they all started laughing.

'Come on Darius, stop mucking about.' They did not believe that I hadn't got through to the final ten. They assumed I was messing around because I was known for making jokes, egging people on and lifting spirits.

I pressed on. 'For those people that have got through, I wish you the best of luck; for those people that didn't get through, we've just got to work harder.'

'Don't joke,' someone said.

'No, I mean it,' I said. Then Michelle realised that I was serious. She ran up to me and hugged me and burst into tears. Before I knew it, people around the room had started to break down.

I've never seen so many boys cry. But I didn't feel like crying myself. I'd already dealt with it and was on to the next thing. I wanted to lighten the mood, so I said, 'Come on guys, don't cry. Can you not feel the love in

'I think you're wrong. It's my dream to have a number-one single as a solo artist and a platinum album by the time I'm thirty-five.'

> *I wanted to lighten the mood so I said, 'Come on guys, don't cry. Can you not feel the love in the room?'*

the room?' I meant it as a light-hearted comment and that's how it was taken – by the other contestants, at least. People started laughing and we all pulled together, then began talking about going out for a meal that night.

They hadn't been crying because I was leaving. But the news that I hadn't got through broke the ice of everybody's emotions – and that ice was so thin that there was suddenly a flood of released tension. But on the show, the voiceover said, 'News that Darius was not going to be in the band left the others devastated,' as the camera zoomed in on loads of tearful faces. It was impossible for the audience to know what was really going on.

I wanted to inspire the others to be strong so I said something like, 'Look, we all have this dream of music. No matter what happens, let's always hold on to that dream and not let this get us down. I believe in music. You should try and hold on to that belief and not give up. Never give up.' After that we all brightened ourselves up, jumped on the bus and went back to our hotel.

Dinner awaited at the Wagamama noodle bar on High Street Kensington, around the corner from the hotel. The only person who wasn't there was Mylene. Nineteen of us sat round one big table, studying the paper menus that also served as place mats. Everyone was making the best of the situation, laughing and joking away, and as I looked on, some simple lyrics began to take form in my mind. *We were strangers at first... But now we're friends in hurt.* I started noting them down on the place mat in front of me and within about twenty minutes I realised that I'd written a little goodbye song. I even had a melody in my head.

Back at the hotel after we had eaten, I said, 'Guys, I want to sing something to you before I go. The last thing that I sang wasn't exactly me. I definitely don't want that final high C to be your lasting impression of me!' So I ran up to my room, grabbed my Gibson, worked out chords, ran downstairs, pulled up a chair from the bar, propped up my guitar...and began to sing.

Instantly the LWT girl looking after us rushed off to get a Steadycam. It was meant to be a private moment and I suddenly became anxious about the context in which I was being filmed. Is this a good or bad thing? I didn't know.

I had lost all perspective. Do I stop singing and tell them not to film it? I asked myself. In the end I continued singing. I figured that the song lyrics were innocent. Anyway, there was nothing they could do now that would reflect badly on me. People were getting into the song and joining in and, although it was making some of them emotional again, there was a very positive atmosphere in the room. It brought us all together in that parting moment, but I couldn't help wishing that the cameras hadn't been there.

On the programme, this was the last you saw of me – singing and playing guitar to my friends while the credits rolled. Ironically, that final shot was the first time I think you actually saw the real me – a glimpse of what I was really about, a flicker of the flame of my passion for music. What's more, I finished writing the song. 'Chrysalis to Butterfly' would eventually become the B-side of 'Colourblind'. That night would prove to be crucial to my motivation to strive and reach my dream of a career in music.

I felt an incredible sense of release. I no longer had this role to play up to, no longer was I trying to please anyone. I was just there, being me. I'd said goodbye to my friends and I was going home. I didn't need to try any more – to try too hard or try to be something I wasn't. The release of pressure gave me back my clarity of thought. I knew what I needed to do. It was time to get my songs together and, more than anything, to focus on being a songwriter. I felt inspired again. I had written a song in twenty minutes and it felt good, it felt right and I felt happy singing it, despite the fact that it was a sad situation.

Afterwards the guys asked if they could sign their names around my lyrics, regardless of the chilli chicken ramen stains. It gave me a feeling that I had been part of something. I've still got that paper mat, folded up, in a drawer at home. Everyone wrote something nice. 'Big D, they keep knocking you down, but you just keep getting on back up' wrote Tony. I was very touched.

sink or swim

I felt lonely in my hotel room that night. I listened to 'I Still Haven't Found What I'm Looking For' by U2. The lyric kept echoing around my head. I thought long and hard about what fame really meant and questioned what exactly it was that I was looking for. What do I really want? I knew that it had never been about being part of a pop group or some commercially driven act. My thoughts kept me up all night. I realised that one of my problems was that I had a desire to be liked – partly because I'd been bullied and unpopular at school. That set me thinking again. My past would fuel my chase of the future, whatever lay in store for me. It didn't matter that a judge didn't like one of my songs – perhaps they did and were criticising it for other reasons – I was happiest when I was writing and singing my own material. As long as I didn't lose sight of that, then everything would work out for the best.

By the time sunlight touched my pillow, I was feeling charged. It had been a great experience, I reasoned. My very first audition and I had got through to the final – not bad at all.

I jumped on the train back to university and made my friends laugh with audition stories. It was a relief to be back in familiar surroundings and I was feeling energised. The audition process had kicked me into gear. It was time to concentrate on songwriting and getting a home studio together.

Three months later the advertising started. Huge billboards went up saying, 'Nigel, pick me!' Teasers flashed on TV screens across the country. People were mystified. 'What the hell is this?' they were asking. I felt like the only person in the whole world who knew what was about to happen. It's started, I thought. Get ready, this is it. But there was absolutely no way I could have prepared myself for the enormous impact that *Popstars* was going to have on my life. I had no idea that a tidal wave was about to hit me…

I felt this incredible sense of release. I no longer had this role to play up to, no longer was I trying to please anyone.

incredible
(what I meant to say)

As I am leaving a Shakespeare lecture at university, a pretty girl approaches me. I haven't seen her around before. She has a beautiful smile. We start chatting about Shakespeare and before I know it we are having a coffee together. She is interesting, animated and articulate, so when she invites me to dinner that night, I think, Good going! You never know, she could even be the girl of my dreams...

When *Popstars* first hit the TV screens three months after the auditions, I was taken aback by how popular it was. From the very start everyone at university was talking about it, asking me questions: 'Who wins? Who gets into the band?' As it happened, I had no idea. We'd all swapped mobile numbers in London, but the final ten's mobiles had changed since then. The five who had been chosen for the band were living in a house in a secret location. The others had signed a contract to say that they wouldn't be in contact with the media.

I watched most of the programmes with my family, at home, and I soon caught on to the fact that they were showing a lot more of me than many of the other contestants. Not surprisingly, they were focusing on the people who were going to be in the finals. I was portrayed as a cocky trouble-maker from the start. I had some sympathetic moments. Whenever someone had done well but been criticised, I would be seen taking them into a corner and saying, 'Look it's all right. They're just being harsh on you because they want you to try harder. Don't take any notice.'

But any moment of saving grace was cut in with what was made to look like fairly annoying behaviour. In one programme there was a shot of me rubbing Jessica's back during the Birmingham auditions. Somehow it came over as a sleazy situation, with the underlying implication that I was trying to worm my way into her affections – when in fact she was a friend by then, complaining of a sore neck. Perhaps it was the voiceover, or the way it was filmed, but even I thought it looked inappropriate when I saw it.

About two weeks into the screening of *Popstars*, my life started to change. Wherever I went, people were looking at me. I began to do a lot of growing up. It was impossible not to question the gap between appearance and reality, because the perception of what had happened at the auditions and what had *really* happened were very different. My father's words echoed in my head. *Not everything is as it appears to be.* I had friends phoning me up saying, 'Darius, what are you like?' People just didn't recognise the person on TV as the guy they knew.

When Popstars first hit the TV screens three months after the auditions, I was taken aback by how popular it was.

incredible

> *I am very stubborn and once I get an idea into my head I can be annoyingly single-minded.*

The more I saw of *Popstars*, the more I began to anticipate my exit from the programme. I wasn't looking forward to it, as you can imagine. But I only had myself to blame if people got the wrong impression of me. Fair enough, I was naïve. I had no idea how I would eventually appear – how was I to know? If I'd been a bit older, more secure in myself and aware of reality TV, I would have approached it differently perhaps. But because there was no precedent to *Popstars* – we didn't live in a post-*Big Brother* era – there was an innocence to the whole proceedings.

Perhaps I wouldn't have thrown myself into it the way that I did. Maybe I would have learned from other people's mistakes. But then we all have to make our own mistakes. I just made mine on national TV! And I'm so glad I went through it. I'm actually very grateful for what happened because it made me see a lot of things in a completely different light. I honestly think that without *Popstars* it would have taken me far longer to appreciate the realities of life. Even though I've always thought that there was some bias in the editing, there were things that I saw myself doing that made me think, Actually there *is* a part of me that I don't like. I am very stubborn and once I get an idea into my head I can be annoyingly single-minded. Although this can work to my advantage, it can also work against me. Because if I haven't reasoned something through properly or I'm working on misinformation, I will still charge forward at 1,000 miles per hour in the wrong direction, knocking everything over as I go.

When it was screened, *Popstars* cleverly appealed to the three elements essential to entertainment – comedy, drama and tragedy. There was the comedy of the initial auditions, of watching the people who couldn't sing, the ones who murdered Mariah Carey songs, hitting bum notes all over the place – but thought they were the best thing since sliced bread. Now that *was* funny. Then there was the drama of who was going to get in, of seeing how people reacted to the trials and tribulations of each round of auditions while under extreme pressure. Finally, there was the tragedy of seeing people you thought would get through, fail; of watching people fall at the final hurdle, after trying so hard and giving everything they had.

I was naïve. I had no idea how I would eventually appear – how was I to know? If I'd been a bit older, more secure in myself and aware of reality TV, I would have approached it differently.

I watched the last show I featured in at home in Glasgow with Mum, Dad and my brothers Aria and Cyrus. My Britney performance was shown in slow motion and edited in with my final interview – they really drew it out. It made you want to laugh at the performance, then you saw the tension on my face during the interview. It seemed to poke fun at me.

They didn't show how long my final session with the judges had been or the progression of what was said. All you saw was the slow-motion version of the last Britney performance edited in with their verdict, 'We do not see you in this pop band,' and my reaction, 'You're wrong.' It made it look as if I was completely lacking in self-awareness. Watching it you might well conclude, What a cocky loser. Who does he think he is? And he reckons he's going to have a number one! Despite this, throughout the programme Mum and Dad kept saying, 'Well done for standing up to them.'

Of course, they didn't and couldn't show me asking Nigel Lythgoe later, after the cameras had stopped rolling, 'What do you really think?'

'Darius,' he said, 'you're too much of an individual to be in a group. You're a solo performer and you know that.' It sounded like he had known it all along.

Oddly enough, when he was interviewed about me a year later, he admitted that my height had been a huge disadvantage. 'He would have had to sit in a chair while everybody else danced around him,' he laughed. Why had I never realised that I was too tall for the group? Looking back, it was obvious that we would have looked silly. The girls only came up to my nipples.

Just before the programme ended, Aria said, 'Don't worry, *Popstars* was only your first attempt. There will be other auditions…' Then just as the closing credits rolled they played my final song 'Chrysalis to Butterfly'. It was weird – there, for the first time, was the real Darius. Suddenly I wished that I'd shown the real me during the whole process.

'Oh, that's a beautiful song,' said Mum.

'When did you write that?' Dad asked.

'Why didn't you sing it earlier?'

'When did you have time to write that one?'

Watching it you might well conclude, What a cocky loser. Who does he think he is?

How do I get up from this? How do you go from being a national joke to achieving your dream?

Suddenly they launched into a full-on conversation, asking questions and talking loudly over me and each other.

I kept my eyes on the TV screen while the wash of words flowed around me. A tear ran down my face, but I didn't want anyone to see. I felt an incredible release of emotion, partly of regret. Why wasn't I like that from the beginning? Why didn't I insist on doing my own material? Then, I could have forged further. I could have made it into the band. I could have made my parents proud. If only I'd been myself...

I went to the bathroom, tidied myself up, walked back into the room and answered my family's questions. I explained that as the programme progressed I realised that no one was taking into consideration the feelings of those who were kicked out. I realised that some had borrowed money, some had left their jobs in the hope that they would be chosen for the group. I felt emotional seeing the uncertainty in their faces as their dreams lay shattered at their feet. It's easy to get knocked down, but to get up and try again is like trying to climb a mountain alone when you can't see the peak. The thought that they might not try again made me sad. It inspired me to write 'Chrysalis to Butterfly'.

Next came the tabloid reaction. Up until then the papers had described me as '*Popstars* Hunk Darius', but come Monday they were full of sneers. I was tagged 'the arrogant loser'. The turnaround gave me a similar feeling to that of being knocked off my feet while playing rugby. I was left winded. Whereas during a rugby match I would always spring straight back up, no matter how tired and cold I felt, there was a moment after *Popstars* when I thought, How do I get up from this? How do you go from being a national joke to achieving your dream?

I wasn't available for comment on the Monday after the programme aired because I was wrapped up doing press to promote *Popstars*. I did TV and radio interviews, as well as an online chat. At the time it was the biggest online interview in the UK, with tens of thousands of people submitting questions. I was so busy that day that some of the papers could not get a quote from me, however hard they tried. So what did they do? A photographer and a journalist turned up at the gates of my brother's primary school to get a quote from him instead – a six-year-old child – as he was waiting for Mum. They shoved a microphone and a lens in his face and asked him, 'So what do you think of your big brother failing in *Popstars*?'

Well, Cyrus took one look at the stranger with the camera, snapping away, ran back into the school and burst into tears. It was a traumatic experience and after that he developed a genuine fear of cameras. For a year he wouldn't let Dad film him on the home video, not even on his birthday.

My father is a respected gastroenterologist who has devoted his life to the NHS. His every waking hour is consumed by saving peoples' lives and making people better. To be distracted from this in any way is very upsetting, but the press came into our lives like a hurricane. Somehow they found his number at work. It rang off the hook with enquiries about me. One journalist even posed as a *patient* to try to get information.

The worst was when my father was performing an operation and received an urgent message concerning 'his son'. Rushing back to his room to receive news, he worried that one of us had had an accident. He burst into his office. 'What has happened?' The man in his room extended his arm for a handshake and smoothly introduced himself as a journalist. 'We're running a feature on Darius, but can't find him for an interview. Would *you* like to make a comment?' Dad hit the roof.

Now Mum is an angel and can't be rude to a soul. It's not in her nature. She is the hardest-working GP I know, and it upset me that the press would never leave her alone. Whenever journalists called, she didn't know how to deal with them. She would spend hours on the phone being polite but trying not to say anything. She had the patience of a saint. It was a bizarre time for all of us because we were a reserved, private family who had been thrown in the deep end.

Some of the stories that appeared over the next few months were just painful. One of the worst was a front page emblazoned with the headline: DARIUS PAYS TO DATE GIRLS! Where did they get that one from? Well, sometime in the months between the *Popstars* auditions and the programme hitting TV screens, I had turned up to the launch of a friend's new company, a dating agency in London called Gorgeous Get Togethers. I took my girlfriend at the time, had a glass of champagne and, just before I left, I was snapped in the background of some of the publicity photographs.

The photo was published in the January issue of a women's magazine –at the height of *Popstars* hysteria – and an observant journalist happened to spot me in the background of the shot. Within no time the paper had contacted Gorgeous Get Togethers. The secretary refused to say anything. But all the journalist needed was confirmation that I had been there. He then persuaded a girl I'd never met to say I'd paid to go on a date with her.

> Some of the stories that appeared over the next few months were just painful.

Unfortunately, this is where the pretty girl who picked me up outside the Shakespeare lecture comes into the story. A couple of hours after I had happily agreed to meet her for dinner that night, I happened to glimpse her getting into a car with a photographer. Well it didn't take a genius to work out that she was a journalist trying to set me up. It was only a week after I'd been seen to leave the programme and the tabloids couldn't get enough of '*Popstars* Loser Darius'. It was a classic case of entrapment. To this day I wonder what it would have been like if I'd turned up to that dinner. I never found out which paper she was from but I imagine she would have quoted me in some 'sensational' exclusive. Luckily I was one step ahead of her. I had already booked the restaurant we were meeting at, where I knew the manager. So I rang and asked him to give her a message when she arrived.

Sorry, can't make it, so don't wait. Dinner's on me. Hope you choke.

I was angry with myself for putting myself and my family in a position where this could happen, I was angry with the press and I was angry with a system that after the first week left me with no support. I had no manager or press agent. I had nobody to guide or advise me in the business. I was on my own.

Fortunately, I found a support and a love that took me by surprise. I started a serious relationship with an amazing girl. I really fell for her. I didn't think it was possible to meet someone whose personality was even more beautiful than her appearance. She was unbelievably caring and supportive of me through all my ups and downs. I don't want to say much more about her though, because I promised her and her parents that I wouldn't drag her into the public gaze.

I had no idea of how to deal with the press. When the tabloids later offered me the chance to tell my story and get paid for it, my first instinct was to have nothing to do with them. So I said, 'I'm thinking about my options,' to anyone who approached me. At one point I foolishly tried to put one paper off by saying that I was considering doing my story with another paper. It fuelled a bidding war and the money they were offering instantly went up to £3,000 or £4,000. To anyone that was a lot of money. It was enough to pay off a student loan. When I mentioned it to my parents, Dad advised, 'If you decide to take any money, make sure you donate it to charity.'

When the tabloids later offered me the chance to tell my story and get paid for it, my first instinct was to have nothing to do with them.

The next day I rang one of the tabloids. 'I'm thinking of doing an interview with you. Would it be possible for you to give me approval over the words that get published?'

The guy at the other end hardly let me finish my sentence.

'Where's the band hiding out?' he asked before he went on to fire a barrage of questions at me.

'I don't know,' I replied.

Within an hour he had faxed me a contract. I rang him back to go through it and again he started firing questions relentlessly.

'Darius, tell us where the band are,' he kept insisting. And I kept saying, 'I don't know where they are. I haven't even been in contact with them.'

'Come on,' he countered. 'Why are you holding out on us?'

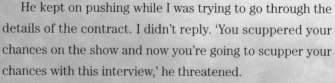

He kept on pushing while I was trying to go through the details of the contract. I didn't reply. 'You scuppered your chances on the show and now you're going to scupper your chances with this interview,' he threatened.

Finally, I lost patience with him.

'Look,' I said, 'I don't know where the band are and I don't particularly want to talk about them. I'd rather talk about my position, my music and my future.'

'I think you're stalling me,' he said accusingly. 'You're going to regret this.' He hung up. I called back several times, but his secretary kept saying that he was in meetings. Then, two days later, the paper reported that *I* had tried to sell them the whereabouts of the band. It was in black and white. But it was a complete lie. I was devastated.

Not long after that, I opened one of the papers to see a picture of me looking really sinister, like the bad guy in a movie. I was shocked to see the words, 'Darius is cult leader'.

My mind flicked back to some press shots I did in Edinburgh to try and raise awareness for a fashion show in aid of a local children's charity. As I posed with a couple of girls in cashmere sweaters on the top of the Balmoral Hotel, one of the photographers shouted, 'Darius, give us a frown!' I hadn't done any modelling, so I just went along with it. But I remember thinking it was weird when he asked me to put my hands behind my back and point my head down, then raise one eyebrow as I looked at the camera. It didn't feel natural to me. But I thought nothing more about it until I saw that very shot being used to illustrate my evil cultish tendencies. It compared me to 'cult leader David Koresh'. It was unbelievable.

As I read on, I came to the ridiculously insignificant quote that had obviously sparked the whole article. '"Darius is lovely," said Kym Marsh. "What an inspiration! We all cried when Darius left. We would have done anything for him. He was like our cult leader."' It was probably a misquote anyway.

I thought nothing more about it until I saw that very shot being used to illustrate my evil cultish tendencies.

I'm sure having a ponytail and goatee didn't help. My appearance was something the newspapers couldn't resist being snide about. Growing my hair had been an act of pure rebellion. My school was a war memorial school where it was compulsory to join one of the cadet forces. I chose the Army and was told I should cut my hair short.

'Why?' I asked.

The answer was, 'Because you have to.'

I've always had an obstinate streak and wanted to do things my way. To this day I hate being told what to do without good reason. If I make a mistake, it's OK, because at least I've tried it my way and I've learned from it. But to be told to do something 'because you have to' doesn't seem good enough for me.

I resented clipping my hair to a number-two grade, so after I left school I didn't cut my hair for three years. Soon it was very long and then I would always just tie it back into a ponytail. I grew a beard but it looked a bit unkempt, so I shaved it, keeping a goatee. It was simply a reaction to leaving school – it wasn't because I liked having long hair or that I was into heavy rock. My mum kept telling me that it was bad for my scalp to wash my hair and sweep it back into a ponytail without drying it, but I couldn't care less about my scalp.

They say that a man hides behind facial hair and it's so true. Back then I think I was. One day I decided to shave my goatee off.

They say that a man hides behind facial hair and it's so true. Back then I think I was hiding. One day I decided to shave my goatee off. Standing in front of the mirror I covered up my chin with my hand and screwed my eyes up so that I could imagine what it would look like skin-coloured, because I couldn't remember. I felt naked and vulnerable. So I changed my mind and kept it. Nobody told me the goatee-and-ponytail combination made me look like cross between a Mafioso from *The Sopranos* and a Greek waiter.

My appearance was so distinctive, even wearing a baseball cap or sunglasses, I was recognised wherever I went. *Popstars* was watched by the nation every Saturday night. I couldn't walk the pavement on any street in Britain without someone shouting at me, 'Where's your number one, Popstar?' and 'Loser!' Trips to the supermarket became an ordeal.

*There was a
window of
opportunity
and I had a
little time
before it
closed.*

I was in a pub one night, waiting for a friend, when this very drunk young guy snarled at me, 'You think you're a tough man, do you, Britney?' Do I stay in this bar now or do I leave? I wondered. It was frustrating when all I wanted was some peace to try and work out what to do with my career. Like I had a career!

One day I got a call from a radio presenter impersonating Nigel Lythgoe. It was around that time that a programme he produced, *Survivor*, was being filmed in Borneo. 'Nigel' was apparently asking me to appear in a new show. At first I was taken in, 'Nigel, how are you?' I said. 'What's this about a new programme you're doing?'

'I'll let Chris Eubank explain,' said the presenter, who then began to speak with a lisp. I soon saw the funny side. I'm not bad at impressions so I played along with it.

But increasingly I had the sense that nobody took me seriously. Nobody really had any idea of who I was. The public had this skewed impression of me and even I had started to dislike the person I came across as in the newspapers. No one realised that I was a musician and a songwriter and that I wanted a career as a recording artist. I was just a guy whose name was always followed by the words: 'whose god-awful rendition of Britney Spear's song "Baby One More Time"'.

I realised that I had to get a demo together so that I could promote my music to record companies. There was a window of opportunity and I had little time before it closed. Although I'd bought the basic equipment to enable me to record music, it would have taken a month to learn how to record a good enough demo – and time was running out. I needed to find a producer who could help me.

I saw London as the creative hub of the music industry. It was where most of the record companies and producers were. So I extended my overdraft and exhausted my student loan, allowing me to take advantage of cheap flights to London. I studied for half the week, then flew down on a Wednesday or Thursday to set up meetings with producers and record companies. I split my time between Edinburgh and London every week for three months. It was exam time, so things were pretty full on. The days were long because every night I'd

Nobody took me seriously. Nobody really had any idea of who I was. The public had this skewed impression of me and even I had started to dislike the person I came across as in the newspapers.

spend hours on the phone to my mum and dad and aunt updating them on developments. That's how my family works!

At first I crashed with friends. I knew a lot of people in London by then. But when I realised this would be happening for a while, I took up the kind offer to stay with my mate Ryan. Little did I know I'd be the third person in a tiny two-bedroom flat. I slept in the kitchen, in the narrow space between the washing machine and tumble dryer – on my back with my knees up. I developed a snore. I had a bad back. And didn't sleep much on 'wash days'. But I had a great friend, a roof over my head, and a bunch of clean clothes.

'One day we'll laugh about this,' I used to joke. We had some fantastic times, despite the cramped living arrangements. I had little money and lived on a diet of bananas, brown bread and beans. The days they offered 'two-for-one' on chicken fillets at the supermarket were the best. I'd cook a simple pasta and chicken dish for both of us and then we'd sit on the little balcony in the sun, drinking discount beer.

I had little money and lived on a diet of bananas, brown bread and beans.

A couple of weeks after my final *Popstars* appearance, I was invited to a debate on the future of pop at the AKA Bar. That morning I'd been on *Big Breakfast* and had had a violent allergic reaction to the powder that had been used on my face. My cheeks swelled up and I had to go to hospital for an antihistamine injection. By the evening, it looked like I had chemical burns on my cheeks.

Nicki Chapman and Paul Adam were on the panel of the debate, along with Culture Club legend Boy George; East 17 and Bros ex-manager Tom Watkins; and one of the most successful A&R guys among the major labels, a man called Simon Cowell. The five *Popstars* finalists who hadn't made it into the winning group Hear'Say were also there.

Boy George was the first to speak. 'How shall we start this thing?' he asked.

'I think we should get a question from the audience,' said Simon Cowell, looking around the room. 'Is Darius here? I'd like to hear a question from Darius.'

I didn't have a record contract and I was risking coming across as a know-it-all.

I was taken by surprise. I didn't know Simon. I didn't know what to say. I blurted out something like, 'In the advent of *Popstars* and bands that are essentially the product of a marketing man's vision, do you not think it's now time for popular music to be written by the artist, produced by the artist and for the artist to be the creative controller?' It was a dangerous thing to say in front of a crowd of music-industry and media people. I had failed to get into the band, I didn't have a record contract and I was risking coming across as a know-it-all.

There was a long pause and then Tom Watkins started laughing. 'Darius, you wouldn't know about originality or songwriting if it smacked you in the face! Go and play with your Britney doll,' he crowed. I felt like I'd been stung, but I didn't react. More than anything I wanted to hear what all these top industry people had to say. While the other *Popstars* contestants were enjoying themselves and having a reunion, I sat and listened carefully to the debate. I was desperate to find out more about the music industry.

Later in the debate Atomic Kitten's manager waxed lyrical about how hard work and self-belief had kept the group going through hard times. Hearing this I thought, I don't care what these people throw at me tonight or tomorrow or any other day. I'm going to work hard and set my sights on my dreams.

When the debate had finished I asked Tom Watkins if he had any advice for me. 'Darius, you need to have a rethink,' he said brusquely, before walking off.

As I was passing Boy George on the stairs, I asked him the same question. 'Go get 'em, kid!' he said encouragingly.

Then I bumped into Simon Cowell. I had never met Simon before. He smiled and gave me his card. 'Give me a call next week and we'll do lunch,' he said smoothly. 'I might have an idea for you.' I was very excited. I had never 'done' lunch before. I knew that he could shift records. And he was interested in me!

I didn't drink any alcohol that night because I wanted a clear head to concentrate on the debate. So I was confused when a waitress kept bringing

me beers. 'No, I'm just on the water,' I kept saying. Then the barman brought me a beer. As he was putting it down, he tried to rest a tray of empty glasses and half-full bottles on my table. At that very moment I turned and in the midst of the crowd could see a lens pointing at me. I stood up instantly, turned my head and walked away from the table. Later on, I approached the photographer, 'What was that about?' Imagine the shot: I'm sitting at a table full of empty drinks, with bright red glowing cheeks. All the photographer needed to do was snap me mid-blink. I could see the headline: 'DARIUS HITS THE BOTTLE!'

I didn't wait for a reply and went to find Michelle, Tony and the rest of my old friends. It was great to see them again. We talked and laughed about audition stories, the bar jostled and the music got louder as the night went on. In the middle of this chaotic scene, a guy in a black leather jacket tapped me on the shoulder. He was in his late forties, with grey stubble, closely cropped hair, piercing blue eyes and a sharp, dignified look. So much had happened that night that I was on edge, hyper-aware and desperately trying to work out who everyone was and what their intentions were. The man gave me his card. I knew there was an agenda just from the way he said my name. 'I don't want to talk here. It's the wrong time. But give me a call and we can talk,' he said, then walked away without even telling me who he was. It was like a scene from a spy film. The card said, 'Nicky Graham, Sony' underlined by a phone number.

Who is he? What is he? What's the deal? I wondered. I phoned him the next day. He told me he was an established producer, working as a consultant for Sony. 'I've been in the business for a long time and worked with people like Bros and Let Loose,' he said. Could this man help me make my dreams come true?

I was on edge, hyper-aware and desperately trying to work out who everyone was and what their intentions were.

mocking bird

'**Y**ou've got a record deal!' says the voice on the other end of the phone.

'What?' I stutter.

'You've got a deal! Sony want to sign you. They love the demo. You've done it!'

I can't believe what I am hearing. It's incredible. Could it possibly be true? I take a deep breath. 'Are you serious?' I ask.

'YES!'

The week after the AKA debate three different potential managers called me. I met up with them all, even though I felt that I would be better to find a producer to make a demo first. I also started making appointments to see record companies.

I decided to research who Simon Cowell was before I met up with him. I found he had sold more records than almost any other A&R man in the country – this man really knew what could sell. But when I dug deeper I found that his successes had included short-term commercial hits, from the Teletubbies to Robson and Jerome. He had turned down opportunities to sign singer-songwriter artists like Craig David and David Gray. I decided not to call him.

I met up with Nicky Graham at his studio. It turned out that he wanted to manage me with his partner, producer Deni Lew. 'Darius, what do you want to do?' he asked. 'What are you about? Play me a song.' So I grabbed my guitar and played for him.

Then I asked him a few questions. 'What's your vibe? Play me what you do.' He played me some striking songs that showed off production values with real depth. He and Deni were developing a band at the time who went on to become Triple 8. Nicky had nurtured them for eighteen months, which proved that he wasn't afraid to put time and effort into a project. Still, he was primarily a producer, not a manager, so I decided to hold out.

Of the remaining potential managers, I eliminated the second, but it took a few meetings and much deliberation. On paper he was perfect, the ex head of A&R at one of the major labels. He was a charmer and he told great anecdotes. But the chemistry just wasn't there between us. I couldn't work out why someone who had been so high up in a record company was now trying to scout bands. Even *I* knew that any advance I might get at this stage in my career wouldn't be very big – and a typical manager's cut (twenty per cent) of something not very big is not very much! So why was he chasing me?

With the third potential manager, I understood why. He had previously managed a successful band in the nineties. We shared the same hometown of Glasgow, so there was an instant link between us. And he was on the tip of something

The chemistry just wasn't there between us. I couldn't work out why someone who had been so high up in a record company was now trying to scout bands.

No amount of money was worth doing something that I thought was selling myself short

that sounded exciting. He was starting afresh having just created the management arm of a respected media promotions company. He knew what was happening in the business minute-to-minute and I picked his brains constantly. But sometimes I felt that he was talking at me, not with me. When I asked him at our first meeting what he was doing in London, his reply didn't exactly inspire confidence. He told me that he wanted to manage the five who didn't make it into Hear'Say, as well as me.

His plan was that he would put together a collection of PAs (public appearances) at nightclubs where I would sing 'Baby One More Time' and one of my own songs. He mentioned a figure of around £80,000 for three months' work. It was an amazing amount of money. But I didn't feel it was right. No amount of money was worth selling myself short and compromising my creative ideas. If I had gone ahead with the PA tour, it would have broken every creative bone in my body and I would have turned into a performing monkey. It wasn't the way to start a career. He saw me as a shortcut to making a fast buck. So I turned him down.

I'm glad I met him though. He introduced me to Judd Lander, an old-school radio plugger and great storyteller, with stories that ran as deep as the laughter lines in his face. Judd was a jack of all trades, doing everything from helping orchestrate the Brits to playing the harmonica solo on 'Karma Chameleon'. (I hadn't realised that Judd was part of my musical education in the eighties!) He was one of the few people I grew to really trust. He believed in me beyond dollar signs. Judd renewed my faith in people's interest in me. I knew one day I'd find a manager who would believe in me like he did.

I didn't want to sign the first management deal that came my way, because everything that had happened to me in the previous few weeks had made me wary. And potential managers were interested in me because of what they had seen on *Popstars*, but they didn't know the real me.

I wanted to turn over every stone, explore every possibility, find the best solution to my dilemma. It was me and my mobile phone. I became a walking-talking office. But the time was ticking away…

Meanwhile the *Popstars* team were making a follow-up programme called *Nearly Popstars*, featuring a few of the contestants who didn't make it into the band. My gut reaction was not to be any part of it. But then I realised that it could be key to raising public awareness of who I really was and what I was trying to achieve, especially if I signed a deal during the filming of the programme. Of course, it didn't turn out that way. Without a manager to represent me or a demo to show what I could do, the record companies weren't exactly sympathetic to my cause.

I remember telling Jamie Nelson, A&R at Parlophone, 'I can sing, I can write, I can play the guitar and I want to do something original. I don't want to do anything manufactured. What can you offer me?'

'What?' he said, with a disbelieving look on his face.

I tried again. 'Are you willing to give me a record deal?'

'That's not how it works,' he laughed. 'For a start, where's your demo?'

As the weeks went on, the sense that time was running out for me grew stronger. When I met Nicky Graham for the second time to talk about management, he said that he had a producer in mind for me. 'He's called Pete Glenister. From what you've played me, I think you guys would work really well together.'

Nicky and Deni drove me to what I first thought was an industrial estate, but in fact was the location of the Music Bank rehearsal studios, where Oasis and the Spice Girls had rehearsed in the past. On the top floor of the warehouse building, we walked into a very lived-in New York-apartment-style recording studio. The room was covered in dust and littered with musical equipment. There were guitars hanging on the walls and a labyrinth of wires on the floor. The couch looked like it was about fifty years old. One corner was filled with cutting-edge production equipment, but everywhere else was organised chaos, infused by the smell of herbal tea and dust. In the middle of the room sat a tall blond man, with grey streaks in his hair and a little goatee below his lip, playing the guitar: Pete Glenister.

Nicky introduced me to Pete, who had an endearingly boyish smile and familiar blue eyes, speckled with laughter lines. There was something about his smile. I felt like I was meeting an old friend. What's more, I felt really at home in his studio.

We started talking about music. I said that I was inspired by Seal and Alanis Morissette. Then we got on to the subject of Trevor Horn, Seal's producer, and the incredible productions that had come out of that relationship. Pete told me that he had been Terence Trent D'Arby's right-hand man, helming Terence's world tour as musical director. He had also produced and written with Alison Moyet and Kirsty MacColl. We talked about our love of classic bands like the Beatles and shared contemporary inspirations like Semisonic. But most importantly, when he played some of his recent material, I was blown away.

I didn't hesitate when Nicky suggested that Pete and I work together. Within a couple of days we were in Nicky's studio with Deni, writing a song. We hit it off and cut a demo quickly. The song we wrote was 'Mocking Bird', which later made it on to my album. (The title is taken from one of my favourite books, *To Kill A Mockingbird*.) It's about a girl in an oppressive relationship with a male figure. We felt that it was important not to make it clear exactly what the relationship was. For me it was very personal, but I didn't want to make that too obvious.

I liked the ambiguity of the Verve song 'The Drugs Don't Work'. On first hearing it is impossible to know that the song is about Richard Ashcroft's mother undergoing chemotherapy. It could just as easily be about heroin or pot addiction. Musically, it's a very different song to 'Mocking Bird', which isn't a ballad, but I put in a reference to the Verve line about the cat in a bag, waiting to drown – *Like a cat held upside down, you'll land feet on the ground* – because I wanted to echo it. 'Mocking Bird' is actually about a girl being abused by her father, but you could easily think that she is being mistreated by her boyfriend or friend or brother or boss.

I knew I was heading in the right direction. Writing 'Mocking Bird' was exhilarating. I was on a high for days afterwards, a feeling that just got better when I got a call from Nicky Graham saying, 'You've got a deal with Sony!' I couldn't believe what I was hearing. Nicky went on to explain that he had played 'Mocking Bird' to the chairman of Sony, and the plan was that it should be the first single. I was over the moon, even though I wasn't sure it was such a good idea to lead with 'Mocking Bird'. Still, I thought, I'm with people I trust. This feels right.

I decided that I wasn't going to ask Nicky to manage me. For me his strengths lay as a producer. I was hoping that there would be a way of keeping Nicky, Pete and Deni as my production team, and that I would find a manager once I had signed with Sony.

But we hit a stumbling block. 'What about your degree?' Mum asked.

'I'll try to defer it,' I replied. 'If the music doesn't work out I'll go back to university.'

I spoke to my tutor in Edinburgh. 'I've been given this opportunity to sign a record deal. Can I defer my degree?'

'I'll look into it,' he said hesitantly. 'I don't know if it's going to be as easy as that.'

He was right. English literature was a course in high demand at Edinburgh. It turned out that if I left university then, a few months before the end of my second year, I would have to start my degree from scratch if I wanted to return. Do not pass 'go', do not collect £200. But if I studied until the end of the academic year, then I could defer and go back into the third year when I was ready. I didn't really have much choice. I told Sony that I was going to have to delay a few months.

Back in Scotland, I couldn't help following the rise and rise of Hear'Say. I

thought 'Pure and Simple' was a pretty standard, if not boring, pop song. The video featured scenes of the band walking towards the camera looking overly styled, with huge balls of fire igniting in the background. In one scene, there is a massive ball of fire behind each one of them and unfortunately their expressions are a bit strained. I was watching with my little brother. 'Cyrus,' I said, 'They're farting fire!' The scene repeated and we burst into laughter. 'That could be you!' Cyrus blurted. We looked at each other and rolled on the ground laughing.

That moment gave me a lot of comfort in the weeks to come.

People were always trying to console me around that time. 'You must be gutted, mate,' they'd say, putting a hand on my shoulder. 'Are you OK?' It was horrible. I felt like shouting, 'No! It's fine! I didn't want to be part of that! Can't you see? Are you all mad?'

I was a figure of fun throughout the nation. You just had to mention my name and people would reel off, 'Can you feel the love in the room?' or laugh hysterically about my Britney performance.

But everyone at university had the record. It was the biggest-selling single of all time and Hear'Say were seen to be a massive success. In fact they were so huge that at one point I couldn't help wondering whether I *should* be wishing I was in the band. Then surely Mum and Dad would stop worrying about me.

The *Nearly Popstars* programme aired. The last thing you saw was me doing the rounds with record companies, not really knowing what I was doing. It made me look like I was chasing after something that wasn't there. The only record company that was taking me seriously at the time was Sony, but I couldn't announce that I was signing with them because it hadn't actually happened yet. I didn't want to scupper my chances. So the programme wasn't great for my image, to say the least. The papers began to take a shot at me again, on the back of the programme, and there was a huge tide of bad publicity against me. I tried to brush it off, not realising how much of an impact it would eventually have.

Because I had been splitting my week between London and Edinburgh, I wasn't seen around at university as much. Everyone had known me as 'social Darius', but suddenly I was nowhere to be seen. I was busy, and when I was around I thought people might not take me seriously. I helped Sean and Simon out organising social and media events in Edinburgh, and still did the phone calls and the legwork, but often I pretended to be Sean on the phone. It was awkward, but it was easier that way. I was just trying to approach things logically. I thought, Well, I don't want any negativity associated with our projects just because I'm involved, and I don't need the hassle.

'Why aren't you fronting things as you would normally do?' asked a girl I was sitting next to at a dinner one night, implying that I was embarrassed or ashamed. I felt ill at ease. Ah, she has a point, I thought. That's how it appears. I was in a horrible situation.

I was a figure of fun throughout the nation. You just had to mention my name and people would reel off, 'Can you feel the love in the room?' or laugh hysterically about my Britney performance. I remember Frank Skinner showing the *Popstars* footage on his show when he interviewed Britney Spears. The audience erupted – and some say that it was the highlight of his series, which I actually take as a compliment. Britney Spears giggled politely, but I don't know what her reaction would have been if the audience hadn't been laughing so much. She was very diplomatic as well. 'You can see he's got his own thing going,' she said. Quite.

It was a strange moment for me, watching Britney Spears watch me. 'Darius, that's the most surreal thing I've seen in my life,' said Aria, who watched me watch Britney watching me. If you'd told me at the time of the *Popstars* auditions that Britney Spears would one day comment on something that I'd done, I wouldn't have believed you.

By the end of that academic year even one of my tutors wasn't taking me seriously, which was painfully frustrating, because I was working hard at university, treading water, trying to keep my head above the surface. With every tutorial came a jibe. One day, he said, 'If you're going to make a contribution, just make sure you don't sing it!'

I was famous without the money to cushion it. I felt helpless and exposed. It worked against me in my social life. It didn't come between me and any of my close friends, but I very quickly came to realise who my real friends were. I could count them on one hand – Sean, Simon, Ryan, Johnnie and my girlfriend. One day I realised I wasn't being invited to parties any more. I was ridiculed wherever I went. It was tough, but I've never admitted it before and I didn't admit it then. I just tried to focus on my work, hoping that the record deal would come off as soon as term finished.

The moment I came out of my end-of-year exams, I told Sony I was ready to sign. But it was too late. The latest wave of press had tipped the balance against me. 'We feel in the light of recent publicity that it's going to be a lot tougher than before…'

It felt like my world had collapsed. Nicky Graham, bless him, bent over backwards to turn things around again. By then he had been hired as special projects A&R at Sony and he was risking his position by pushing it as far as he did. He tried to motivate the company at different levels, persuading people to support me and help to get me a deal, and at various times I was very near to making it happen. I had the backing of the

I was famous without the money to cushion it. I felt helpless and exposed. It worked against me in my social life.

head of A&R, but in the end the deal collapsed. I was back where I had been several months before – no deal, no manager. It was a huge disappointment.

I felt like a failure. I'd been turned down by *Popstars* as well as by Sony – and as soon as Sony turned me down, there was no way that any of the other majors would give me a deal. That's the way it works in the music industry. It's very rare for an artist to be turned down by a major label and then snapped up by another.

At the forefront of my mind I knew I needed a manager. But the more I thought about my management dilemma, the more I felt like I was banging my head against a wall. I remember thinking, If there's anyone who can manage me, it's my dad, even though he knows nothing about the music industry!

Aware of their connections in the entertainment world, Dad suggested that we ask his sister, my Auntie Ashraf, and her husband, Uncle Harold, if they knew anyone that could help. They in turn suggested that I meet up with their good friend John.

'Who's John?' I asked.

John Simpson was a top sports manager working within the international entertainment management company CSS Stella. He had worked with everyone from Tiger Woods to Ayrton Senna. More importantly, he was a friend of the family.

John picked me up from Ryan's and took me straight to his family home, where I met his wife and kids. I instantly warmed to him. John was an educated, charming man with a quick wit and a devilish sense of humour. He had an air of dignity that struck me. He was a family man. I thought, I wouldn't care if he didn't know a thing about the music industry. I've only just met him and I trust this man.

I thought, I wouldn't care if he didn't know a thing about the music industry. I've only just met him and I trust this man.

'I'll look after you,' he said at the end of the evening. I breathed a huge sigh of relief. It felt like John had lifted a great weight from my chest. Those were the words that I wanted to hear more than anything else. I had waited so long, but finally I had found my manager.

I learned so much from John Simpson and the wonderful woman he worked with – Tracy Chapman – who went on to manage my day-to-day schedule. I think Tracy was heaven-sent. Intelligent, elegant and bubblier than champagne, she swept into my life like an angel. Despite the negative publicity about me, I was being requested to do things left, right and centre. John and Tracy weathered the storm with me and protected me; they dealt with all my media requests and helped me prioritise everything.

But when it came to my appearance at the Glasgow roadshow, the 35,000-strong crowd of Live and Loud, I didn't ask for their help. As my manager, John was getting twenty per cent of nothing. I reasoned he was doing so much for me that I felt it was only fair that I organise this gig myself. I had arranged it before I'd even met John, not long after *Popstars* was aired, so I placed the responsibility firmly on my own shoulders.

Back in Edinburgh I managed to throw a group of musicians together at the very last minute. We were all broke and I had to lend my guitar to my guitarist because he couldn't afford his own. Most of the band were doing it for nothing but the ride, which was very good of them. I covered petrol and any money I could spare was going to a bass player I'd met earlier in the year at the Tron. He was an amazing American session musician who had played with legends – from Chaka Khan to Stevie Wonder. It was great to have him on board.

I was billed to play 'Mocking Bird'. The first chance I had to go through it with the band was on the morning of the gig. Our feet did not hit the ground. Sean drove me to Glasgow in his battered Ford Escort, a burgundy dust-bucket that was fast falling apart. He brought along his camera to take some shots of me on stage and of his girlfriend, who was doing backing vocals. The others travelled in a thirty-year-old ambulance that had been bought for £500 the week before.

I hadn't been able to eat all day because of nerves. In fact I was so nervous that it was impossible to concentrate on giving Sean directions to the gig site, Bellahouston Park. The stress levels in the car rose so high that suddenly I broke out into nervous laughter. Then we all started laughing hysterically and before we knew it the sign for the gig had appeared. What a relief.

We drove up to the back gates. As we pulled up, a security man approached the car. 'Where are your parking permits?' he asked. My heart sank. I'd organised everything myself and I hadn't thought to ask about things like parking permits. We didn't have any of the right passes or stickers and Sean and I spent the next hour trying to sort all the administration out.

The security guys sneered when the ambulance pulled up. 'Is this your entourage? Where's your manager?' they laughed. They thought I was a complete joke. Later on one of them shouted at Sean for taking photos without a press pass and almost broke his camera as he ripped out the film and threw it on the floor.

I was standing by the ambulance when a white limo with blacked-out windows drew up. Out bundled the members of Hear'Say. 'Hey guys, how's it going?' I said, but as I went to shake Danny's hand a burly security guard in a bomber jacket and dark glasses forcefully pushed me out of the way. Mylene and Suzanne appeared to ignore me as they walked past. Kym threw a glance back at me, smiled and mouthed the words, 'I'm sorry'. It was weird, a very public snubbing. The next minute Hear'Say were swept up on to the stage to perform 'Pure and Simple'. The applause was rapturous.

Later, boy band Five arrived in stretch tour cars with black-outs and silver alloys. They had a bodyguard each, masseurs, a chef and a group of at least a dozen dancers. They ran on stage and ran off, then rushed away to be flown to the next gig by private jet. If you'd told me in that blaze of frantic movement that they would soon split, I would eventually turn down a record deal from the man who created Five, then go on to secure my own deal, I would have laughed in disbelief. It was in such stark contrast to where I was at the time. But at that moment I thought, I never want to be like that. I never want to be in a position where I've got so many people round me that I'm impossible to approach. Remembering that now, I try to be as accessible to my fans as possible.

Amidst all the chaos backstage, I had a sudden moment of clarity. I needed to talk with Sean, so I grabbed him and said, 'Let's go to the car.' Sean, bless him, was rushed off his feet trying to help organise things for me, and I could see that he was disheartened on my behalf. In the car I said, 'Sean, let's promise each other one thing – let's never forget today and promise we will never treat anyone in the way that we've been treated.'

We vowed to stay determined whoever criticised us, and to make it in our prospective careers – Sean in film and me in music. We shook on it. Backstage I changed in the rain behind the toilets – the dressing rooms were reserved for

I never want to be in a position where I've got so many people round me that I'm impossible to approach.

Time was definitely running out. My golden opportunity had turned to silver. Everyone kept telling me that the window was closing. It was an intense time.

'stars' and their entourage. 'Thank you for being such a good friend,' I said. 'One day, in years to come, we will look back on this and laugh.' Little did I know that it would be only one year before I secured a record deal and Sean flew off to Hong Kong to work for Columbia Pictures.

Although there was some applause, I heard some booing as I walked on stage to my home crowd. I stood dazed, lost in the moment. The noises washed over me. Heckled by distant, blurred faces, I could see the love and encouragement in the expression on my mum's face as she stood in the rain at the front of the crowd. Suddenly I regained focus. Something amazing happened as I sang 'Mocking Bird'. By the end of the song the booing had stopped and I actually received some muffled applause and cheers.

Half an hour after I came off stage I went to find Hear'Say to pass on my congratulations. I didn't get to speak to them. They were too busy doing interviews in the green room.

So in many ways it was a disheartening day, but I stayed motivated by chanting positive phrases in my head, You've performed a song that you believe in, in front of 35,000 people, with amazing musicians. You've got fantastic friends. Your parents are out there in the crowd and even if everyone else was booing you, it doesn't matter because the people close to you love you. And they love this song.

Not long after Live and Loud my manager John introduced me to his good friend Barry Mason, who had co-written some of Tom Jones' biggest hits, including 'Delilah'. I met up with Barry at his family home and couldn't fail to notice all the platinum discs on the wall. I thought he was a lovely man and he was totally on it, very sharp. He had just set up Xenex, an independent record company, and teamed up with a songwriting production team.

John suggested that I write a song with the team Barry had suggested. They were very encouraging when I played them my compositions. I even played them 'Chrysalis to Butterfly', the song that I had written on my last night of the *Popstars* auditions. They said they loved it. 'It's good enough to make it on to the album.'

'But Darius,' they said, 'we need a tried and trusted hit, something that sticks to a proven formula. We like your songs but they might be a bit too clever for a single.'

I started playing something simpler and catchier but they stopped me halfway through the first chorus. 'Wait, we've got an idea for a song. Listen to this.' They put on a track called 'Gun To My Head' and started singing along to it. 'This is the song that will launch your career! You should co-write the rest of the album yourself, but we need to get a single out quickly and this is it!'

I instantly latched on to the lyric which was all about making sure other people allow you the space to do your own thing. It was what I'd been trying to say to everyone all along! The next thing I knew John Simpson was saying, 'What a great song! You should really record this! Let's try and get into a studio as soon as possible.'

Time was definitely running out. My golden opportunity had turned to silver. Everyone kept telling me that the window was closing. It was an intense time. I had a recurring dream that kept turning into a symbolic nightmare. I would be standing in the lower part of an hourglass while grains of sand filtered down from above. I would desperately try to get out but I couldn't. Slowly the sand would rise up to my neck. Eventually it would reach my head. I could physically feel it. I'd wake up gasping. I couldn't breathe!

To complicate things, Nicky Graham suddenly hit me with the news that the deal with Sony was back on the cards. They had changed their minds. The contract would be in writing when the key player at Sony got back from holiday. At the same time I was being pressured to record 'Gun To My Head'. I felt like a rag doll being pulled by both arms and both legs – and the head too. In the end I decided to record 'Gun To My Head' because I was promised that, if I did, I would then be able to write an album of my own songs.

Barry Mason sent over a letter of intention. 'They want to do a full twelve-thousand-pound production of "Gun To My Head",' John explained. He went on to detail that I would be liable for the bill if it wasn't released. This was not unusual. But I only had twenty-four hours to make up my mind.

Twelve thousand pounds! 'Why can't I do a demo?' I asked, feeling a deep sense of panic.

'Xenex want to run with this now. If you do a demo, it just means that you will have to go back into the studio and do it all again later. They think you're running out of time. It's a take-it-or-leave-it offer.'

I felt like a rag doll being pulled by both arms and both legs – and the head too.

I tried to make sense of my predicament. If I recorded 'Gun to my Head' but then didn't release it because the Sony deal came through, I'd be able to pay back the recording cost out of my Sony advance. But if Sony didn't offer me a contract, at least I'd still have the prospect of a record deal with Xenex, and not be left with two doors closed. It's going to cost me £12,000 to keep this door open though, I thought. It was more money than I could imagine. I felt the strain bear down on me and was still worried about the effect all this was having on my parents, who I felt I had let down. So I recorded the song.

The plan was to use an established producer, who would give the record a distinctive, contemporary feel. But when I turned up to the studio in Wimbledon I was instead introduced to a guy who was really an engineer trying to make it in production. That was the first compromise of the day. I didn't say anything, but as I was singing the lyric about being your own person, I suddenly realised the irony of my situation. Actually, this is not what I'm about!

When I heard the track back, including a long electric-guitar solo, I felt that it sounded dated. I asked if it could be cut in a more modern way. They compromised and made some changes. But it still wasn't right.

Xenex went ahead and offered me a deal, saying that I had to sign within a week or lose £12,000. They wanted a concrete commitment from me. The Sony deal still hadn't arrived, but Nicky kept assuring me that it was on its way.

The week passed and there was still no sign of the Sony contract, but the deadline for signing the Xenex deal was nearly up. On the Friday I sat in John Simpson's office, knowing that I had to make a decision. 'Do you believe in what I'm doing?' I asked John. 'Do you believe that I have the talent to make it?'

There was a long pause. 'Absolutely,' said John.

'Well John, as my manager, can you buffer this offer for me? If Xenex want me, they'll wait a week. Simple as that.'

So John negotiated a delay on the deadline until the following Friday. The weekend passed, Monday came and the Sony deal still did not arrive. Nicky said there had been some kind of problem with the lawyers. I knew this kind of thing could happen, so I went on weighing up my options. Nicky promised the Sony contract would arrive by the end of play Friday – 'no ifs or buts' – the same day as the new deadline with Xenex.

On the Friday, the Xenex team turned up at John's office with a contract. Barry Mason was there, with the songwriting team and the investor. I sat down with them and tried to focus. The Sony deal was only a possibility, but the Xenex deal was there in front of me. The investor then talked to me for fifteen minutes about how he believed in me, and that he was putting a lot of money into this project.

'Can you not see what you're doing?' I asked him. 'The song is called "Gun To My Head" and that's exactly the stand-off I'm facing.'

I drew the meeting out for an hour in the increasingly elusive hope that the Sony contract could suddenly arrive. It hit 5.30p.m. Xenex signed their half of the contract and I just sat there with a large silver-ringed black fountain pen in my hand. It felt unusually heavy; my palms were sweating. Everyone's eyes were on me, waiting for me to sign this piece of paper. The only person who wouldn't catch my eye was John's PA, Tracy Chapman.

At the last minute, I put the pen down. 'I'm sorry. I can't do this,' I said. I stood up, walked out and went straight to the bathroom. I looked at myself in the mirror and said, 'You've made the right decision.' I then walked back into the room, shook everyone by the hand and said, 'One day it will all make sense, but I just couldn't do this now.'

I was left with nothing. In fact, I was left with less than nothing because I had a £12,000 debt to pay off. I also felt like I'd let my manager down. John was a wonderful, magnanimous man, but he must have felt a deep sense of frustration at this point. He had tried his best to make something happen for me and it must have looked like I'd thrown it back in his face, although I really hoped he didn't see it that way. Things couldn't get any worse – or so I thought. Even at that point I had no idea how low it is possible for a person to go. But although I didn't know it, I was about to drop right down to the very bottom, like a broken, wrecked ship in the middle of a deep and stormy sea.

I was left with nothing. In fact, I was left with less than nothing because I had a £12,000 debt to pay off.

chapter six

better
than that

I walk into the audition room with my guitar. The floor

is wooden and there are mirrors lining the walls.

Nigel Lythgoe, Nicki Chapman and Simon Cowell are

sitting behind a desk, frowning at me. I pick up my guitar

and start singing 'Colourblind'. When it's over, I silently

stand there, waiting for a reaction. 'Is that it?' says Nigel.

'That was possibly the worst performance I've ever

seen.' The judges start to rip me apart. I haven't got

through. I'm a failure.

Every night I have the same nightmare.

I needed to get hold of £12,000 quickly. Where was I going to find that sort of money? My dad had offered to vouch for me but I couldn't burden him like that. But I was desperate, so the following Monday I phoned the guy who had wanted me do a series of PAs after *Popstars*, to find out if there was a way of doing these without performing 'Baby One More Time'. I didn't care if I only earned a fraction of the £80,000 he had originally mentioned, but he didn't go for it.

I'd been offered some television work and, although I wasn't interested in TV presenting, I agreed to front a programme called *TV To Die For*, subtitled 'The greatest musical moments in TV history'. It was too well-paid to turn it down. Unbelievably, my Britney performance was up in the top ten, along with the Beatles singing 'All You Need Is Love' and a clip of Bob Marley in concert. I was two places down from Band Aid! The world must have gone mad...

One of the set-ups was supposed to illustrate the excesses of the rock-and-roll lifestyle. As I sat in a Jacuzzi full of bubble bath, along with two Playboy models and a dwarf with a snorkel and mask on, I delivered my line and thought, What the hell am I doing here? *TV To Die For* seemed like a good thing to do because it helped pay my debts, but afterwards I realised that I really needed to focus on the music. The PA guy still wanted to work with me even though John Simpson was managing me. He left me messages saying, 'I can help make you big.'

I really didn't know how to approach tackling the record companies after being turned down by Sony again and I wondered whether John would mind if this guy helped out in the role of my 'music agent'. John met up with him and they agreed that he would work on setting up record company meetings for me. He also organised a gig at the G-A-Y club night at the Astoria in London.

I turned up to G-A-Y with Christian, a great guitarist who was a friend of Deni Lew, and three friends from Triple 8, who were helping on backing vocals. We were excited. It was going to be fun. But when we arrived at the Astoria, I was told that he had agreed for the gig to be billed as Darius's 'official final performance of "Baby One More Time"'. I was appalled. I didn't want to do it but I couldn't pull out. The flyers had gone out and the posters were up. I had to stick by what had been agreed.

I sat in a Jacuzzi full of bubble bath, along with two Playboy models and a dwarf with a snorkel and mask on...

The 'music agent' had previously assured me that I was going to go down a storm. Never has anyone been so wrong. I walked on stage to boos and heckles. As I started into 'Baby One More Time', a bottle flew at me. I stepped out of its way and continued singing. Coins came next, denting my guitar.

I noticed three girls make their way from the back of the room to the front. Soon they were standing in front of the stage, watching and listening, ignoring the boos and laughter. I'm going to get through this, I thought. I'm going to sing for those three girls.

Then I felt spit on my face. It reminded me of the time I was beaten up and spat on as a boy. I honestly thought I was going to be sick right there. By the time I sang 'Sticks and Stones', my own song, saliva was dripping from my face.

One of the girls at the front caught my attention. She looked deep into my eyes and I stared back, mesmerised. There was an instant connection between the two of us. 'Keep going. It's going to be all right,' she mouthed. So I did. She had appeared out of nowhere in the crowd and, although I didn't see her again to thank her, I'll never forget her face.

That night at G-A-Y was the toughest thing I've ever had to do. I felt so embarrassed. I had simultaneous urges to run away, cry, scream, shout and explode. I wanted to tell everyone that this wasn't what I was about. I wanted the audience to listen to my lyrics and change their minds about me. I didn't understand why people hated me. It wasn't dislike. It was a genuine hatred. It was a really extreme reaction.

Booking me for G-A-Y had been a disaster. G-A-Y is a celebration of being who you are and not trying to be something that you are not – and there was I, hiding behind this stupid ponytail and goatee, not looking particularly proud of what I was doing. The way the G-A-Y clubbers reacted to me gave me a real insight into how I appeared, although that didn't help me at the time. Someone out there was trying to tell me that I needed to change. I had to stop bowing to other people's ideas of what I should be or do and start following my heart. I still have the guitar with the mark made by a flying coin that reminds me of that night.

Then I felt spit on my face. It reminded me of the time I was beaten up and spat on as a boy.

I wanted the audience to listen to my lyrics and change their minds about me. I didn't understand why people hated me. It wasn't dislike. It was a genuine hatred. It was a really extreme reaction.

After chasing me for so long, and all I'd been through at G-A-Y, my 'music agent' ended up pulling out. I have never felt so let down in my life.

It wasn't long after that night that I hit rock bottom. Back in Edinburgh, I stopped taking care of myself and grew a beard. I didn't go out and I became very pale. My face had a stunned look about it, partly as a result of my recurring nightmares about people throwing coins and spitting at me on stage. I was racked with doubts about myself and what people thought of me. I couldn't stop kicking myself. How could I have been so stupid and naïve? How could I have let myself make such big mistakes publicly?

I was foolish to base my self-image on what was being projected at me by people I didn't know. My family still loved me; my friends were still there for me. It was just that I couldn't see it. I began to drink to escape. I drank from lunchtime onwards. At 12.30p.m. I'd meet the guys at the pub and have a couple of pints. At 2p.m. I would go to meet a friend at one of a string of bars and student hang-outs between the student campus and the Royal Mile. At 6p.m. I'd arrange to meet other people I knew. There was always someone to drink with. At 8p.m. I would turn up at Sean and Simon's flat on the Royal Mile, asking if they wanted to come to the Tron, not realising that I was already drunk.

The Tron was a bar popular with students, just off the Royal Mile. Originally an Irish pub, there would always be great live Celtic music upstairs, with a fiddler, a guitarist and a drummer. I loved it. It was where I had performed a couple of open-mike gigs during my first year. But I went from seeing the place as a creative hive to seeing it as a place of escape, where I could get my fix of oblivion. I didn't want to play my guitar downstairs any more and I wasn't interested in the Celtic band. That was background music now.

A lot of the time I didn't seem drunk. I was good at hiding it – and I could drink a lot because I have a high metabolism, I was active and fit. Soon I could knock back a good few drinks and they wouldn't even register. Then, as I built up a tolerance, I found myself drinking more and more, day-in, day-out. I was going back to my flat on the other side of town at ten or eleven at night, drinking

How could I have been so stupid and naïve? How could I have let myself make such big mistakes publicly?

I had tried to push all my emotions and passion for music and for life to the very back of my mind.

with my flatmates, passing out in the early hours of the morning and sleeping in 'til midday. The next day I would meet the guys for lunch and start the whole process over again.

I didn't go home to Glasgow nearly as much at weekends. I'd phone Mum and Dad making excuses and saying I was busy, when in fact I was just out drinking. I didn't want them to know how unhappy I was. I couldn't look them in the eye. If I had, they would have instantly known that something was very wrong and I couldn't bear the thought of the worry it would cause them. I'd already put them through so much stress with the media.

I put my parents off whenever they wanted to come over with Aria and Cyrus. Once they turned up at the flat to surprise me and I didn't answer the door. A little later they called me and left a message – 'We're here!' They called again in the evening but I didn't get back to them. It was awful behaviour. I feel ashamed when I think of it.

Sean and Simon soon realised what was going on because I was turning up at their flat in progressively embarrassing states. I think it was tough for them to see me trying to cope with all the venom that was being directed at me, from the press and people in the street. They tried to get me to open up but I couldn't. Finally they sat me down one day and said, 'Darius, what are you doing? What is happening?'

I was shocked when they confronted me. I couldn't see what the problem was. Surely they understood that I wanted to forget, put the past behind me and stop feeling? I had tried to push all my emotions and passion for music and for life to the very back of my mind. I yearned for numbness. But confronted by Sean and Simon's worried faces, I knew that I couldn't pretend any more. I broke down in front of them. Then they broke down too.

That night was a turning point for me. Talking to Sean and Simon allowed me to acknowledge the situation I was in. I didn't have to pretend everything was all right any more. It was time to face my demons and sort myself out.

I went back home to Mum and Dad. We talked and talked and talked. My brother Aria was very insightful. I'm so close to him that it's almost like having a twin and he seemed to understand all the things that I couldn't articulate. He was amazingly supportive and reassuring.

It was Aria's suggestion that I go and stay with Auntie Ashraf and Uncle Harold in Derbyshire. My aunt is an amazing woman, I've always been very close to her. She is a Reiki master, very spiritual and wise, and a bit like a second mother. Uncle Harold is a well-known artist and a fascinating, witty, worldly wise man. They are both very loving and caring. So I left my guitar in Glasgow, put my CDs beside the rubbish and went off into the middle of nowhere to get away from the press and bars and alcohol. I didn't want to listen to music or play the guitar. I was looking for peace.

Those weeks were very restful. I withdrew into myself. I read books, went for walks, ate well and slept a lot. Uncle Harold took me for long drives through the countryside and talked to me about the challenges and pressures that an artist faces. Some of the things he said really made sense to me and helped shed light on my situation. Auntie Ashraf taught me Reiki and meditation. Now I can heal myself and others, although I'm not allowed to teach Reiki. I began to pray. I began listening to music again. Auntie Ashraf's record collection included Labi Siffre, T-Rex, Simon and Garfunkel and the Beatles. My time in Derbyshire was escapism of a much purer form than the drinking had been. It was the start of my regeneration.

When I returned to Glasgow, I watched the *Popstars* tapes again and tried to learn from what I was seeing. What happened there? I'd think. That didn't happen – oh dear, that *did* happen. When I'd finished with them I packed them away in the attic.

A couple of days later I turned on the radio for the first time in ages. Travis were singing, 'Why Does It Always Rain On Me?' The lyric struck me as really funny in a dark way and I laughed hard. There was a desperation in my laughter though. Immediately afterwards Coldplay's 'Trouble' came on. *They spun a web for me*, sang Chris Martin, over and over again. I don't know who he was singing about, but I related to those words. Suddenly I had this image of myself flying along, all over the place, oblivious to the spider's web in front of me. I'd flown smack bang into the centre of it and the more I struggled, the more entangled I became. I realised that it was time to stop fighting and accept my situation. I'm here now. How do I disentangle myself?

Next was 'Here Comes The Sun' by the Beatles. The melody washed over me; the lyric warmed my soul. I'd forgotten how powerful music could be. I thought, How wonderful that a song can affect you so much!

Luckily Aria had saved the box of CDs that I had put out for the binmen, so I pulled out all three songs and listened to them on repeat. And I thought, I want to write songs like that. I want to write songs that make me feel good. I want to write songs that touch people. Late that night I found myself jotting down some ideas, snapshots of the different feelings I'd had in my relationships with girls. I related each feeling to a colour. Feeling red – angry; feeling green – jealous. It was elementary stuff, but it seemed to work. Gradually a melody began to take form in my head. Wow, I thought, I'm recovering. It was a huge relief. The song would go on to be my first hit single, 'Colourblind'.

When I told my parents, friends and family that I was thinking of trying out for Pop Idol, they thought I was crazy.

Then, one day during the summer holidays, someone on the radio started talking about a new TV talent search. Later the same day I walked into WH Smith and saw a leaflet about it. Then I heard someone talking about it in the local newsagent. What is this? I thought. The fact that I've heard about it three times in a day has got to be telling me something. There wasn't that much information available. All anyone seemed to know was that it was a solo audition and the winner would be given a record deal.

I found out that the programme was being produced by some of the same team who produced *Popstars*. This time it was a solo competition on a much bigger scale – *Pop Idol*. My brain told me to steer well clear of it – I would be asking for trouble – but my gut instinct was to go for it. I knew it would be tough trying again, but something told me that it was the right way forward.

Nigel Lythgoe was producing *Pop Idol* and Nicki Chapman was set to be one of the judges, so I tried to contact them at 19 Entertainment, where they both now worked, to ask their advice about whether I should enter.

When I told my parents, friends and family that I was thinking of trying out for *Pop Idol*, they thought I was crazy. Mum cried and my father said, 'I don't think that would be wise.' My friends

I found myself jotting down some ideas, snapshots of the different feelings I'd had in my relationships with girls. I related each to a colour. Feeling red – angry; feeling green – jealousy. It was elementary stuff, but it seemed to work.

thought I had a screw loose. Their reaction was as if I was telling them that I wanted to do Britney all over again. Aria, thank goodness, was a bit more diplomatic. 'Darius, you will always do what you need to do. You don't need to ask anyone,' he said.

'If I hadn't been in *Popstars*, you'd be encouraging me to audition,' I protested to my parents. I felt that the advice from those closest to me was tainted by love. They could not be objective because their perspective was skewed by what had gone before. Even Pete and Deni thought it was a bad idea and I could see it was enough to make John Simpson pull his hair out. Nobody could see it the way I did.

'But this is the right thing to do!' I insisted. 'I can't tell you why, but it just feels right.'

'It'll be the end of you,' they all said.

I just needed one person to say yes and that would have been enough for me. It wasn't about chasing fame or money. I saw *Pop Idol* as an opportunity to show people who I really was, to follow my dream. It was a chance to redeem myself and make a fresh start. I figured that probably the only people who could give me objective advice were Nigel Lythgoe and Nicki Chapman. I was sure that they would give me an honest and informed answer.

'If I ask them whether I should audition – as a kid who wants to make it in music – and they say yes, will you support me?' I asked Mum and Dad. Understandably, my parents were frightened for me. They worried about the effect it would have on me if things went wrong again. We had a very long conversation about it and the upshot of it was that they said, 'OK, we will support you, but only if Nicki and Nigel approve.'

I chased Nigel Lythgoe the length and breadth of the country – literally. When I found out that he was going to be in Birmingham, I jumped on a train straight there. All I needed was to see him face to face and ask, 'Should I do this?' But when I turned up to the studios where he was supposed to be, I'd missed him by a few minutes.

I knew that his next port of call was Edinburgh, where he was judging at the Edinburgh Festival comedy awards. I jumped on another train. Again I was too late. I went back to my flat, called his office in London and left a message.

'I've just missed Nigel Lythgoe. Can you tell him I'm in the area and would love to see him?'

A few minutes later my mobile phone rang. 'Hello Darius, this is Nigel Lythgoe.' For a split second I thought it might be another prank call from a radio station. Yeah, pull the other one. Then I realised that it really was him. It was a long time since I'd heard his voice, so it was quite surreal speaking to him.

I laid my cards on the table. 'Do you think I should try for *Pop Idol*?'

'Darius, this is a tough one,' he replied. 'If you hadn't auditioned for *Popstars*, I'd say absolutely. But if you now audition for this, you will be eaten up.'

My stomach was in my mouth as I heard this. I felt sick. But I thanked him, jokily apologised for stalking him – he laughingly called me a 'persistent

bugger' – and hung up. It was awful, because I then began questioning whether Nigel might have any motive for keeping me off the programme. If so, what was it? If there was a rule that barred anyone who had auditioned on a programme like this before, he would have said so. If there was a political obstacle, he would have underlined it. So what else could it be? I couldn't think of anything. In fact, I reasoned that it would be in his interests for me to make an appearance because it would mean an extra little snippet in *Heat*

magazine. 'The magic moment when Darius got booted off a TV show. Again!' There was nothing for it but to accept that there was no ulterior motive. He was giving me his honest opinion: to save me from myself. It left a very sour taste. Never mind, I thought, turning my attention to Nicki Chapman. Nicki will tell me that it's a good idea.

Over the next few days, I got to know the receptionist at 19 Management extremely well. By the fourth day I was chatting and flirting with her as if I was trying for a date. Finally she put me through to Nicki Chapman. The relief was enormous. It had almost got to the stage where I had forgotten why I was calling.

'It's difficult for me to speak to you,' said Nicki.

'I understand, but I just need to ask you one thing and please, just give me your honest opinion. Should I do this? Should I audition for this programme?'

There was a long pause. When Nicki next spoke, her tone had changed completely. 'Darius, I think you are setting yourself up for the biggest fall that you could ever have.' I was completely taken aback. 'The media will have a field day,' she continued. 'They will lap up the fact that you're there. But look, whatever happens, this is the last time that I can speak to you until I see you again, if I ever see you again.'

She started to say goodbye. 'One thing, before you go,' I interjected. 'If I turn up to the Glasgow audition, can I come with a guitar and sing my own song?'

'I don't think there is anything against it in the rules,' she said. 'But nobody has turned up with an instrument yet.' Then she added, 'Darius, my advice would be to disappear for three years, maybe four. If you really are a good songwriter, you'll come back with good material and maybe you can change people's idea of you through music.'

I put the phone down. Dad came downstairs. I had told him to listen in on the extension because I was sure that Nicki would tell me that it was a good idea to enter *Pop Idol*. He had heard everything.

So ten days before the Glasgow audition, I told my parents, 'I respect your judgement and I'm going to follow your advice. I won't do the audition. I'll go back to university, finish my degree and become the best songwriter that I possibly can.'

I couldn't sleep that night. Every time I dozed off I plunged into a nightmare about singing 'Colourblind' in front of Nigel, Nicki and Simon. 'Is that it?' Nigel would say in the dream, when I had finished playing. 'That was perhaps the worst performance I've ever seen.' Then the judges would tear into me. Their comments echoed and repeated in my head until I woke up in a cold sweat, feeling terrified. I was frightened by the idea of watching a panel of judges react to the song that had pulled me from a dark place and helped me focus on my dream. Singing 'Colourblind' was baring my soul. It wasn't hard to imagine them saying, 'Sorry, it's not even good enough to get you through the first round.'

Every night I had the same nightmare. It drove me nuts. One night Mum woke up and came downstairs to find me drinking hot chocolate in the kitchen. 'What's wrong?' she

'Darius, I think you are setting yourself up for the biggest fall that you could ever have.'

asked. She gave me a motherly cuddle, the kind that enveloped me and made me feel safe. It didn't console me this time though – and you know that something is really wrong when even a hug from your own mother can't help you.

The Glasgow audition was getting closer. I became limp, lifeless and despondent. I didn't go out. I wasn't eating properly, which isn't like me because I usually eat like a horse. I sat on the sofa for days on end, watching Aria come in and out of the house, start one summer job, get fired, start another. On the morning of the audition I sat miserably at the kitchen table, playing with a bowl of cereal. I kept attacking it with my spoon, stabbing it until it was just a revolting mush. Aria, freshly shaved and smart, walked into the kitchen, looked at me and said, 'What *is* wrong with you?'

I mumbled something about the Glasgow audition. 'Darius,' he said, 'if you apply for a job and don't get it, does that mean that you just stop applying?' With that, he walked out of the room and left the house.

He's right! I thought. I felt a surge of adrenaline run through me. I rushed upstairs to find Mum and Dad. 'I can't explain it, but I have a feeling in my gut that I feel I must follow. If I don't, I'll be haunted by "what if" for the rest of my life. Can I just have your blind support on this one thing?' I asked. 'I promise I will never ask you for it again, but I can't do this without your support.'

Mum hugged me and Dad gave me his blessing.

I looked at my watch. Oh God! The audition had probably started already. I ran upstairs, looked at myself in the mirror and said, 'Come on!' Then I tried a motivational technique that Auntie Ashraf had told me about and stared into my own eyes, almost behind my reflection, trying to visualise fire.

I was about to set sail again. Threatening clouds hung in the sky. The forecast wasn't good, but something told me that I had to make this journey. Far ahead on the horizon I was sure I could see sunshine. I stepped off the shore. Where would I land this time?

The Glasgow audition was getting closer. I became limp, lifeless and despondent. I didn't go out. I wasn't eating properly, which isn't like me because I usually eat like a horse.

simple like the truth

It's 10p.m. and I'm sitting on the sofa in our hotel suite. I've had the phone pressed to my ear for nearly an hour.

'If I win, I'm turning down their offer of a record deal,' I tell my father.

'What? Are you crazy?' He sounds aghast.

'If they don't let me write my own songs then I'm not going to sign with them.'

'But legally you can't pull out!' says Dad.

He's got a point. I am locked into a contract and there's nothing I can do about it. Or is there?

It was the height of heat in August and I had no idea where to go when I arrived at the Scottish Exhibition Centre, where the Glasgow audition for *Pop Idol* was held. It's a huge place and I rushed around in a frantic panic. Then I spotted a big group of pop hopefuls lining up outside one of the halls. There was a buzz in the crowd as I approached. Out of nowhere a girl came up and asked me for my autograph. 'Look, it's Darius!' a couple of other girls shouted. 'Can we have a photo with you?' I was amazed.

I made my way to the administration table, picked up an entry form and was sent outside to fill it in. 'Describe yourself in five words,' it said at the bottom.

'Can't believe I'm doing this,' I wrote.

As I walked back into the building, I noticed that a camera had been set up in the lobby. 'Pretend we're not here,' said the cameraman. Here I go again, I thought.

I was directed to a room downstairs. The camera followed me. Ant and Dec greeted me and we had a bit of banter. Then Dec said, 'So, are you going to hit us, baby, one more time then, Darius?' There was a silence. It was an awkward moment. I gave Dec a look and I could tell that he thought I was offended. Then I smiled. I was just playing with him.

'Phew!' said Dec, 'I thought you really were going to hit me there.'

I sat patiently waiting outside the audition room, visualising the bright lights and cameras and table of judges behind the door. When I was called, I picked up my guitar. 'Leave your guitar out here,' said one of the production assistants. Something inside me told me not to cause a fuss. So I left my guitar outside. The first thing I saw when I walked through the door was the *Pop Idol* logo painted on the floor. It brought to mind a cheesy sixties disco. I looked around the room at the lights, cameras, sound equipment and logos. It was obvious that this was a much bigger project than *Popstars*.

I thought it would be rude not to introduce myself. Although I'd met Simon Cowell six months before and I already knew Nicki Chapman, Pete Waterman was new to me. Of course I was aware of who he was. I'd listened to Kylie and all the great Stock, Aitken and Waterman hits in the late eighties. Neil Fox wasn't there because he had his regular slot on Capital FM to fill.

I was asked to sing a song. 'May I play my guitar?' I asked. 'I would like to sing a song I've written because I think it would best demonstrate my ability as a songwriter and solo artist.'

Nicki Chapman said, 'Sure.' Pete Waterman and Simon Cowell said, 'Of course.' But just as I was leaving the room – at the very moment that my hand was reaching for the door handle – a voice boomed out. 'Sorry, we don't have clearance for that.' I felt a shudder go through me. It sounded uncannily like Nigel Lythgoe's voice. I was rooted to the spot and couldn't move. What is happening? I thought.

Sure enough, I turned round to see Nigel emerge from behind one of the cameras. I hadn't seen him before because of the bright lights. 'Nobody else has been allowed to play an instrument and so Darius can't either,' he said. He didn't address me; he just talked as if I wasn't there.

Simon Cowell and Nigel Lythgoe proceeded to have an argument about it. Things started to get heated. I just stood there in amazement. I was shocked. I've caused chaos before I've even had a chance to sing a note! I thought.

The argument suddenly came to a halt. 'Simon, we will talk about this later,' said Nigel. 'Darius, leave the room, come back in and ask what you asked again.' I did as I was told. Oh no, it's for the cameras, I thought. I left the room then walked back in, my palms sweaty, dread in my stomach. 'I'd like to be given the opportunity to play the guitar and sing a song that I've written because I feel that it would best demonstrate my ability as a solo performer,' I said.

'No, Darius, nobody else has been allowed to,' said Simon Cowell, expressionlessly. 'If you'd like to sing a song we all know, please proceed.'

I looked at Nicki Chapman but couldn't catch her eye. What am I going to do? I thought in a panic. Part of my reason for auditioning had just gone out of the window. But I couldn't just walk out. As if I hadn't already been branded as an arrogant loser! If I walked out then my forehead would be branded with an 'L' for the rest of my life. I had to think on my feet. So I sang the last song I had heard – in the car on the way to the audition – 'Future Love Paradise' by Seal. I sang it off the top of my head. I didn't even know if I'd started in the right key.

'Nobody else has been allowed to play an instrument and so Darius can't either.'

I was half-expecting Simon Cowell to say, 'Darius, that was perhaps the worst performance I have ever seen.' Instead, Nicki Chapman got in first and said it was great. Pete Waterman said, 'Boy, you've got a voice on you!' Simon Cowell said, 'Darius, I'll reserve judgement on this one, but you're through.'

Someone later told me that Nigel hadn't allowed me to sing a song I'd written to save me the embarrassment of being criticised by Simon Cowell. At the time I thought he was deliberately blocking me, but I now wonder whether in fact he was actually being kind.

Back home, Cyrus and I got into one of our wrestling matches. As he jumped me from behind, he grabbed onto my hair and yanked my head back. 'It's not a tree branch!' I yelled. 'That hurts!'

That night, as I went to kiss him goodnight, he opened his eyes and squinted up at me. 'What's wrong?' I asked. He looked quite upset. 'Are you all right?'

'Darius, you're rough!' he replied.

I put my hand to my face. 'I suppose I am,' I answered.

For the rest of the evening I couldn't stop feeling my face. Why have I got this ghastly facial hair? I wondered to myself. I shaved it off the next morning, with Cyrus standing beside me. Later in the day I had my hair cut short. It was like shedding a skin.

The *Pop Idol* callbacks were in London and we all stayed at the Marriott Hotel in Maida Vale. Over the next few days we would be whittled down from one hundred contestants to fifty. I met Will Young and Gareth Gates on the first day. Will struck me as one of the most down-to-earth people you could ever meet: well spoken, polite, articulate and gentle. He was always wearing what we called the 'grandad cap' and hand-knitted golfing jumpers. Will wasn't a big showman, but he had a truly solid and rich voice and was technically one of the best singers. Because of this, I think he was judged mainly on his voice, whereas a lot of the other characters were judged as a package, which was interesting.

I got on with Gareth from the start. Although we were in a room full of people, I couldn't help noticing the handsome guy with gelled spiky hair in a

Why have I got this ghastly facial hair? I wondered to myself. I shaved it off the next morning...

shiny grey-blue two-tone suit and polished black shoes. He was the only guy in a suit, which I thought was great. He and his mum approached me as I was sitting on a leather couch, waiting for instructions from the judges. We shook hands and had a chat. I warmed to him quickly.

Gareth told me that he really respected me for entering *Pop Idol*. 'People got you wrong on *Popstars*,' he said. I think he was looking for a bit of reassurance, so we sat on the couch and talked for a while. I remember thinking that he was very much someone with a dream. His mum was very supportive of him. That night I talked to her about the Gates family in the laundry room of the hotel, while she was pressing Gareth's suit and I ironed my shirt.

During a break in the auditions at the Criterion Theatre in Piccadilly the next day, Gareth and I sat cross-legged on the floor in the bar and started jamming with our guitars. Before we knew it there was a crowd of people joining in or listening. Then I started playing 'More Than Words' by Extreme, a simple ballad that had really struck a chord with me when I first heard it at the age of twelve. I'll never forget how it made the hairs on the back of my neck stand up. It was the song that originally inspired me to play the guitar and write a song. I still get shivers whenever I hear it.

It was the song that originally inspired me to play the guitar and write a song. I still get shivers whenever I hear it.

'I know that one!' said Gareth and he started playing along. I noticed that he played it slightly differently. I couldn't quite put my finger on it, but his version sounded a lot choppier, much more pop.

'How do you know that song?' I asked when we'd finished.

'It's a Westlife song on their second album,' he replied.

I was surprised. Not that he didn't know the original but that I'd had no idea that Westlife had covered it.

On *Pop Idol* there were no silly dance routines to learn and the cameras didn't follow you into the toilets. But there were some similarities with *Popstars*. The atmosphere on the second day, when the final seventy were being whittled down to the final fifty, was a real reminder of that tense afternoon at the Birmingham *Popstars* callbacks.

It was 11 September 2001. An hour before the audition, I'd turned on the television in my hotel room and seen the shocking Twin Towers footage. Back

simple like the truth

at the Criterion Theatre, I tried to take in the enormity of what I had witnessed. It hadn't really sunk in for a lot of people. We all had to stand in line on stage while names were called out. If you heard your name, you had to step forward, not knowing if the people in the front line or the back line had got through. Then the contestants in the front line were told that they had got through. Suddenly people were jumping and screaming and celebrating.

I remember standing stock-still and seeing this scene in what seemed like slow motion. Although I was among the winners in the front line, I felt numb. The world has gone mad, I thought. How can we celebrate getting through an audition when the Twin Towers have just collapsed? I looked around me. This is just a game, I thought, a silly TV programme. So no matter what happens here, I'm not going to get affected by it.

I had made it to the final fifty. But to proceed with this next leg of the assault course, all contestants had to certify that they were not engaged in any management or recording contract prior to *Pop Idol*. Legally, any existing contract would prevent a contestant from signing with 19 Entertainment and BMG records should they make it to the final stage. I was stumped. After everything they had done for me, it was ironic that my management with CSS Stellar was the only thing holding me back. I explained my predicament to them. Their reaction was gracious and understanding. 'I only ever want the best for you,' John Simpson told me. CSS released me of my management contract. I was ready to pounce over whatever the next hurdle might be.

The following round of auditions were held at Elstree Studios in November. The final fifty were divided into five groups of ten and each week the programme focused on one of the groups. The two contestants from each group with the highest number of votes from the general public made it into the *Pop Idol* finals. Rik Waller, Aaron Bayley and Sarah Whatmore were in my group, so I knew I was going to have a tough time getting through. After two days of intensive rehearsals with the musical team, we recorded the show on Wednesday 28 November. Live voting took place after the broadcast of the show the following Saturday.

I sang 'Something Inside So Strong' by Labi Siffre – a favourite of my parents' and a song I have always loved. I was pleased with my performance, but when it

Although I was among the winners in the front line, I felt numb. The world has gone mad, I thought. How can we celebrate getting through an audition when the Twin Towers have just collapsed?

came down to the vote, Rik and Aaron got through into the finals and I came third, with Sarah Whatmore just behind me. Aaron had beaten me by a fraction of one per cent. I was out.

My disappointment was brief and fleeting. You could see that it wasn't a show of bravado, even though I was aware that my reaction was being broadcast live. I watched the figures come up on screen and my heart sank for a minute. Then I thought, Oh well, what another great little episode in my life. Time to move on to the next one. I was far more detached from the process than I had been during *Popstars*. To be honest, all I could think about was writing songs and making a demo of 'Colourblind'. I was desperate to get into the studio again. I didn't even want to hang around to be interviewed by Ant and Dec. Earlier, I'd had an idea for a new song and I needed to get my hands on a guitar as soon as possible.

I was far more detached from the process than I had been during Popstars.

I went back to university, intending to fly down to London as often as I could to work on the demo of 'Colourblind' with Pete Glenister, who wanted to go on writing with me even though I still didn't have a record deal. He was doing it in good faith because he believed in me, which was encouraging. I was finally moving closer to making my dreams a reality.

So I didn't know what to think when I got a call a couple of weeks later. I was asked if I would like to take place in the *Pop Idol* finals, because Rik Waller was ill. I thought it had to be a joke. It took a few minutes before I established that it wasn't. Statistically I had come the closest after the final ten to getting into the finals, so I was Rik's logical replacement. It was back to London again.

My phone rang as I arrived at the Marriott. 'Bad news, I'm afraid,' said Nigel Lythgoe, who went on to explain that the show was legally bound to give Rik a week's grace in which to get better. If he was able to sing by the following week, then he would be allowed back on the show – and I would be sent back to Glasgow. In the meantime I just had to wait it out.

Rik's leaving the show was all very mysterious and there has been lots of speculation about it. After he left we heard he had signed a deal with Liberty Records, part of EMI, and then he released his single. It was the wrong decision, in my opinion. Instead of going out gracefully, he belly flopped. And there was no water left in the pool afterwards.

I hung around in London while this was going on, hearing all kinds of rumours about Rik signing a deal, but not knowing if they were true. The production team saw me through that week. My emotions were yo-yoing and one of them said to me, 'I can't believe we're putting you through this. It's not fair. I'm so sorry. It's out of our control.' Then at the end of the week the news came through that Rik was definitely out. I was set to join the other eight finalists on the next show. I was so happy. I could hardly believe my luck.

For the next seven weeks I lived and breathed *Pop Idol*. There was a great camaraderie on and off set and no sense of competition. We were all rooting for each other, which was odd, but wonderful. Our schedule of interviews, filming, music and performance rehearsals was relentless, but I remember feeling quite relaxed about the whole thing. When I was kicked off the show at the final-fifty stage, I had lost my desire to win – and it never returned. It was simply like getting a bonus credit at the arcade when you're a kid. I was playing for free and it was fun.

When I got through the first week I almost fell off my seat. I had turned up to the Fountain Studios in Wembley thinking, Hello everybody, I'm here to sing one more song, certain that I would be voted off. Feeling that I didn't really deserve to be in the final, that I was there by the skin of my teeth, I had decided just to have a great time. It was a brilliant opportunity to sing one of my favourite songs on national TV and have a laugh with it. I was glad just to be there. You could see it in my smile.

There was a Christmas theme to the show and I sang the Johnny Mathis song 'When A Child Is Born'. It was my first live TV performance and I was very nervous before I went on. Even though things had gone well in the dress and technical rehearsals, you just never know what might happen on live TV. I needn't have worried. The minute I started singing I totally forgot that I was being watched by millions of people, which was actually something I found very hard to imagine anyway.

Afterwards, Pete Waterman was full of praise. 'Darius, you're a national institution – you're better known than the Queen Mother – and you sang that song in a way that would have made Johnny Mathis proud.'

When I was kicked off the show at the final-fifty stage I had lost my desire to win – and it never returned.

The next week I sang 'What The World Needs Now'. The excitement of singing live was incredible. It was the same feeling as being on stage at my first school gig, only more intense. I felt naked in front of the audience. It was a strange sensation and it partly inspired the line *I feel naked in your eyes* in 'Gotta Know Tonight', the seventh track on my album. Again I couldn't believe that I hadn't been voted off. It was the same the following week when I sang 'I Have A Dream' by Abba. I felt so lucky to have the chance to go on doing what I loved. It was such a buzz preparing for each performance and then coming off stage riding such a high.

At the final-six stage, Will and I, Rosie Ribbons and Hayley Evetts moved into a suite at the Marriott. It had four bedrooms, a communal living room and a kitchen. Gareth and Zoe Birkett had their own rooms because they were under eighteen. Will and I spent many evenings lounging around on the couches in our suite, talking into the early hours. We were living in a bubble, being driven everywhere, often working sixteen hours a day. There was a huge wall between us and the outside world and none of us realised the full impact *Pop Idol* was having on the country until we left the show.

The idea that I could win hadn't even entered my head. But by the time that I got to the final five and it occurred to me that I actually had a chance, I realised that I didn't actually want to. I told my father that if it came to that, I wouldn't sign a deal unless I was given the go-ahead to write my own songs. Dad pointed out that I was locked into a contract, but in my mind my principles were stronger than any contract. I would rather be sued than sing covers. I really believed that my fate was to release 'Colourblind' and nothing was going to shake me off course.

It was obvious who Simon Cowell's favourite was. So many times he said to Gareth in his appraisals, 'Gareth, You *are* a pop idol'. Well there's nothing subliminal in that message to the audience. It seemed to me that he was saying, 'This guy is the one.'

He and Pete Waterman had a huge argument over me in the final-five week. The theme of the show on 19 January was 'Big Band Night' and I sang the Nat King Cole classic 'Let's Face The Music And Dance'.

> *There was a huge wall between us and the outside world and none of us realised the real impact Pop Idol was having on the country*

'I think that was the weakest performance tonight, I'm afraid,' said Simon Cowell when I'd finished. 'For some reason I just didn't find that believable. I just didn't get it.'

The audience started booing. Next up was Nicki Chapman.

'When you first came into this search, I really wasn't sure about you. But each week you've improved your performances and everything else too. You're doing a tremendous job.'

There were huge cheers at this.

Neil Fox then said, 'Standing there, you couldn't be more different from the guy that sang "Baby One More Time", could you?' The crowd erupted. Pete Waterman had to shout to be heard over them.

'Simon, you must have something in your ears, mate, because that was as close as I've ever heard to Nat King Cole in my life.' Simon Cowell tried to interrupt, but Pete wouldn't let him speak. 'His vocals tonight were brilliant. He is amazing. You can't say that was bad!' he went on.

The audience were going mad. 'Can I just say,' I said above the noise, 'thank you for your comments. One of the reasons I'm here is to get your criticisms. They're constructive. But Simon, I think perhaps you should bring your waistband down a notch because it might be restricting the blood flow to your head.'

The crowd were on their feet. I hadn't prepared what I'd said. It came off the cuff and I almost tripped up over my words as I was saying them. I thought maybe I'd pushed it a bit far poking fun at Simon's famous high-waisted trousers, but the audience reaction egged me on. They loved it.

Having the guts to say something like that was a real sign of my growing confidence. It was like when you windsurf for the first time in high winds and waves, using a sinker board. A sinker board isn't designed to float, so when you first try it you need to have faith in your ability to manipulate the sail so that you catch enough wind to support you. In the same way, I was still finding faith in my own abilities as a performer and learning to stand up for myself. I'd been wiped out by a big wave before, but now I was rising to the crest.

Later in the programme, a woman from the audience stood up and asked Simon Cowell a question. 'As the commercial

'...Simon I think perhaps you should bring your waistband down a notch because it might be restricting the blood flow to your head.'

simple like the truth

record producer on this show, did you consciously try and bias the viewers against Darius tonight because you didn't want him to win?'

That started Pete and Simon off again. 'No, you've always got to give an honest opinion,' Simon replied to the questioner. Pete began to defend me again. 'I've watched this kid grow and I think he sang that song tonight as well as Nat King Cole,' he said emphatically. It was an incredible compliment, but I have to say I was amazed that they were getting so worked up over me. The argument became more and more intense, until Ant and Dec had to break it up with a joke about putting the two of them in a boxing ring and watching them slug it out on cable TV.

The selection process for the songs we sang varied from week to week. Usually we submitted a list of songs, one or two of which would be selected. On 26 January the theme was 'number-one songs' and I sang 'It's Not Unusual' by Tom Jones and Atomic Kitten's 'Whole Again'. I had to fight to sing 'It's Not

Unusual', though. At first it was rejected, but I put my foot down. I wanted to sing something that would appeal to people. It was wicked fun. The crowd went wild when I took a leaf out of Tom Jones's book and threw in a hip shake. That was the week that I felt I had finally turned public opinion around.

I first noticed a change in the public's perception of me after the programme featuring the first Glasgow audition was screened in early October. I got the impression that people originally thought I was there for some kind of set-up or joke. They couldn't understand why I would be there after all the ridicule I'd gone through. The act of turning up and auditioning again made them question what they knew of me, I think. And gradually people began to re-evaluate me. When I came back clean shaven and without my ponytail, I sensed that people associated the change in image with a change in who I was. In fact the change had started before I cut my hair and was still going on. And although I looked younger, I was definitely older.

I was still positive that each week would be my last, however, so I was shocked when I got into the final three. It was another weatherman moment. Oh dear, I really have got a chance of winning, I thought. But I don't want to win!

The *Sun* and GMTV did their own polls predicting who was going to be chucked off the show each week and they got it right every time bar one. When it came to the final three they all said that Will would go out, I would

I got the impression that people originally thought I was there as some kind of set-up or joke. They couldn't understand why I would be there after all the ridicule I'd gone through.'

come second and Gareth would win. In fact it was Will who went on to win the competition, and I think that took a lot of people by surprise.

For the final three shows, we were given 'freedom of choice' on one song and the second song was chosen for us. It just so happened that they gave Gareth 'Unchained Melody' to sing, which had been covered a few years previously by Simon Cowell's artists Robson and Jerome. Coincidentally, it also happens to be Gareth's favourite song. Will made his own choice because they couldn't think of a song to suit his range. And I was hoping to sing 'You've Lost That Lovin' Feeling' by the Righteous Brothers, a song I've always loved, which demonstrated my range well, from low to high. I definitely felt that I could do it justice. When Ray Monk, our musical director, first heard me sing it, he told everyone, 'This is Darius's best song. It's going to blow them away when he sings it on Saturday.'

But I was told not to sing it. 'Well, what would you have me sing?' I asked. I nearly laughed when the answer came back, 'Never Gonna Give You Up' by Rick Astley. It was a joke. I really didn't get it.

That same week, Will, Gareth and I were sent to Olympic Studios to record 'Evergreen' and 'Anything is Possible' which would be released as a double 'A' side single by the *Pop Idol* winner the week after the final show. Because of production deadlines we all had to vocal both songs three weeks before the winner was decided. That way, no matter who won, the single would be ready for immediate release.

When I got into the studio, I was confused to find that both songs had been arranged in the same key for all of us. My voice has a bass range, Will is a tenor and Gareth is a high tenor or alto – and you don't get a bass singing what an alto or a high tenor voice would sing.

'I can't sing these notes,' I explained. 'They're simply not in my range.'

The producers seemed embarrassed. 'Well Darius, you can always change some notes,' they suggested. It was silly. Changing notes would have meant essentially changing the structure of the song, and wouldn't have worked. It's not only not ideal, it's just not what you would do professionally.

'Is there no way of transposing it to the right key?' I asked.

'No, this is the version of the song you all have to sing to,' they replied.

I simply couldn't sing some of the notes. I thought, Perhaps people aren't expecting me to win. In which case, I thought, it was just as well that I didn't want to win.

Could this man be any more patronising? I thought. I was furious.

They sent cameras in to film us recording the songs, which really increased the pressure. It was tense. This gauntlet was being watched by an audience.

'I don't think I can sing this. It's not in my range,' I said politely to Simon Cowell on camera.

He instantly went into executive-producer mode. 'Darius,' he said, 'I believe that you are a good enough singer to sing this song. You've just got to try and not give up.' The irony of this comment smacked me in the face. Could this man be any more patronising? I thought. I was furious. I really wanted to let rip and it was a struggle to keep my temper.

Back at the Olympic Studios with Ray Monk the next day, I sang 'You've Lost That Lovin' Feeling' again. 'This is your song,' said Ray excitedly. 'If anyone can cover this song, it's you.'

Simon Cowell turned up. 'I hear you've been causing trouble again,' he said. 'What is it this time?'

I explained that I didn't feel that 'Never Gonna Give You Up' reflected what kind of singer I was. 'I feel it's only fair that you give me a song that matches my range and suits me as an artist,' I added.

I sang 'You've Lost That Lovin' Feeling' to him and, without blowing my own trumpet, I knew that I had nailed it. Ray Monk gave me a big smile when I'd finished. Simon Cowell, on the other hand, crossed his arms and said, 'You know, Darius, when you sing that song, I just don't buy it.'

'What is it you don't buy, me or the song?' I asked.

'No, you're not singing that. I've got to go,' he said, walking out.

Later I had a face-off with him off camera. 'There's no way I'm singing 'Never Gonna Give You Up', I said. 'If you try to make me, I won't do the show.'

In the end I sang the Walker Brothers song 'Make It Easy On Yourself', which was the nearest thing I could find to 'You've Lost That Lovin' Feeling', although it was less well-known. That was the week I was voted off and there was a nice symmetry in the fact that the very last words I sang on the show were, *So breaking up is so very hard to do, so very hard to do.*

I was very happy to come third, considering that I had got into the final ten by default and hadn't expected to stay for more than one show. I didn't want to have to release someone else's songs, so I was glad I didn't win . I was ready to go. In a strange way it was a relief. I just wanted to see my family.

That night my parents and I met Simon Fuller for the first time. The founder of 19 Entertainment, he was the genius behind the Spice Girls phenomenon, pop brand S Club and the true *Pop Idol* maestro. My mother and father spoke at length with him while I finished a barrage of interviews. Simon said to me, 'I don't think since David Beckham has anyone turned round their fortunes in such a way. And you did it without help from management or PR. It's extraordinary.' It was such an encouraging thing to say and the fact that he said it in front of my parents made the night feel special.

Simon went on to explain that he thought I had a future in music and had an idea about how I could be managed. He told me about Nick Godwyn, who had promoted the Spice Girls and Annie Lennox, and since formed a joint-venture management company with Simon – Brilliant 19. It was possible that they could manage me together, Simon fulfilling a more executive role. It was an amazing offer and seemed like a way forward.

The following day I met Nick Godwyn for the first time. I wanted to know what my parents' thought of him, so they went with me. Nick was a diamond. His quick, dry wit caught me off-guard and made me laugh, and Mum immediately warmed to him – which is always a good sign. He came across as a patient man, calmly responding with real depth of thought to a series of questions reeled off at him. I liked Nick. He was understated, and I imagined that no matter how hard times might get, there would always be hope in his eyes.

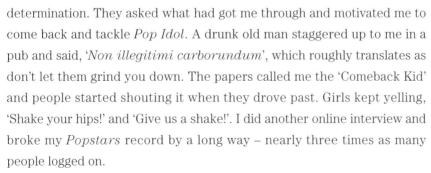

Life was different after *Pop Idol*. People started approaching me in the street to say how much they admired my determination. They asked what had got me through and motivated me to come back and tackle *Pop Idol*. A drunk old man staggered up to me in a pub and said, '*Non illegitimi carborundum*', which roughly translates as don't let them grind you down. The papers called me the 'Comeback Kid' and people started shouting it when they drove past. Girls kept yelling, 'Shake your hips!' and 'Give us a shake!'. I did another online interview and broke my *Popstars* record by a long way – nearly three times as many people logged on.

When the series was over, I was told that Simon Cowell wanted a meeting with me. Apparently he was going to offer me a deal. I went to meet him at his

simple like the truth

offices. Bizarrely, there was a power cut when I arrived, so he suggested that we have the meeting at his flat in Holland Park instead.

Holland Park is a beautiful area of London and the Edwardian building we drew up at looked stunning from the outside. So I was taken aback by the minimalist interior of Simon's flat. Newly renovated, with marble floors and curved, polished plaster walls, it didn't feel lived in. There was something empty about it.

'Simon, you really need a woman in your life to spruce this place up,' I said. He laughed.

'You need a big Persian rug, flowers and paintings on the walls. What's up?'

'Darius, this is the ultimate bachelor pad, set out for ultimate convenience,' he boasted. He was right. But it felt soulless.

He poured some drinks and we sat down and started talking about music. 'What exactly do you propose?' I asked him.

'Well, we have a contract with all ten of you. Will won, but we also have the right to sign you, and any of the final ten. I'm offering Gareth a record deal.'

What was the point of winning then? I thought. There's no real prize if you get a recording contract by coming second or third. The next minute he said, 'I want to sign you as well,' hitting me with figures that I wouldn't have believed a year before. I was overwhelmed. I passed him a demo of 'Colourblind' and said, 'I'd really like you to hear this song.'

He threw it on the table. 'Don't worry about these things. I've got a bunch of songs that are proven hits. And I know this may come as a surprise, but I've thought about it and in my opinion the right song to launch your career is "You've Lost That Lovin' Feeling".'

I was stunned. I couldn't believe it. Yeah, pull the other one, it's got bells on, I thought. I half-expected a man with a camera to come from around the corner at that point, saying, 'Got you!'

Simon went on to explain that he had in mind a double 'A' side of 'You've Lost That Lovin' Feeling' and 'It's Not Unusual'. 'We'll compile the album from covers as well as songs that suit your range, written by professional songwriters.'

I tried to bring the conversation back to 'Colourblind'. 'Don't you want to listen to—'

'Don't worry about that,' he cut in. 'Darius, you're a star and I can make you a millionaire. I can master this project with my eyes closed.'

'I want to bring something creative to the music business.'

First his flat had brought to mind *The Devil's Advocate*. Now he was beginning to resemble Al Pacino's character in my mind. In the film, Pacino offers Keanu Reeves the world if he will agree to sell his soul.

'Simon, I want to work with someone who is passionate about my music,' I said, feeling shocked and disappointed. I had to persuade him to see things my way because I wasn't allowed to turn down his offer. I was locked into a contract. Simon continued, 'And I know exactly who should produce your first single – Pete Waterman.'

He got on the phone to Pete Waterman and said, 'Darius is coming to see you on Monday. I think you should produce "You've Lost That Lovin' Feeling".' And that was pretty much the end of the meeting.

I realised I had to find some way of getting out of the situation I was in. I was tied into something that prevented me fulfilling my dreams as a singer-songwriter. It was a tricky one. It was a sticky situation. I didn't know what to do. It occurred to me that it might be a big mistake to turn down a deal from such a brilliant businessman. I respected Simon because I believed he would achieve anything he set out to do. But I didn't want to make a career out of singing covers. What's more, I wanted a record company that would invest in me and promote me as a priority, where I didn't want to compete with Will or Gareth. That weekend I really struggled.

So when Monday came and I walked into Pete Waterman's office, I wasn't feeling my best. Pete noticed immediately that something was wrong. 'How are you, son?' he asked. 'You look shaken.' He was always so warm and lovely towards me. 'You're not happy, are you?' he said.

I was honest with him. 'I want to do something original,' I said. 'I want to bring something creative to the music business. I want to entertain people with something new.'

There was a long pause. 'You're right,' he said, looking at me with real intensity. Then he walked over to his stereo, picked up a CD and put it on. A beautiful ballad began to play. Even though I was listening to a demo version, using a session singer, I found it melodically haunting. About halfway through the song, Pete pressed pause. 'Darius,' he said, 'You've got the chance to do something special, something different. Don't let it slip through your fingers.'

I had no idea where any of this was leading. 'I believe in you, kid,' he went on. 'You can set this place alight and hang around to see the fire for a long

time. But you've got to make the right decision now, because everyone's got an agenda, kid.'

He pressed play, the song continued. I can't remember all the lyrics but the chorus was striking in its simplicity and it was all about appreciating what you have. It really got to me. Forget the fame and money and big deals, I thought. All I need is my friends, family and guitar. All I want is to sing and create and write music. By the end of the song, I had tears streaming down my face. I looked up at Pete and noticed that his face was red. He had taken off his glasses, his head was in his hands and there were tears in his eyes. There was a real connection between us at that moment. Then, a few seconds later, he said, 'Enough of that,' and began to talk about my future again.

'If you want to do something original, I want to do it with you,' he went on. Suddenly there was a light at the end of the tunnel. Could Pete Waterman turn out to be my saviour? I remembered that his record company was funded by Jive Records, who have Britney Spears on their books. Now that really would be coming full circle, I thought.

By the end of that week Dad had flown down to meet Pete. They got on famously. And I felt safe with Pete. He was very reassuring. Over the next couple of weeks, I met up with him quite a few times. He told me his life story, we got to know each other and became mates. I respected him; I still respect him. But then one day he said to me, 'We have to get a song on the shelves. We should really have got it out last week, let alone next week, and we need something that is ready to release now. Do you remember that ballad I played you? That is the song to launch your career. It had you and me in tears; imagine what it's going to do if you release it.'

He played the song again and for a minute I tried to imagine singing it. At least it wasn't a cover, I thought. Then I came to my senses.

'But Pete, I'm a songwriter. I want to be part of the music so that when people buy my records they are listening to my thoughts and words, not someone else's.'

I played him 'Colourblind'. He sat there, motionless, But then I saw him tapping his foot underneath his desk. Then he said, 'Kid, let me tell you. You're a great singer, but you've got a lot to learn about songwriting. It doesn't matter because I'll let you contribute on the album, but when it comes to the songs, you've got to leave the ball in my court.'

It was a smack in the face, because we had talked so much about wanting to do something real, about making a difference. It was 'Gun to my Head' time again. I was thrown. I just wanted to hear something simple, like the truth.

'So Pete, do you not think it's a good song?'

'No, kid,' he said. I couldn't believe what he was telling me. I believed in this song. 'But don't worry about that,' he went on, 'I want you to sign to me.' I never thought it would happen – I'd met a man who was as persistent as I was. But hold on a minute, I thought, I'm jumping from the frying pan into the fire. It was very confusing.

Luckily, the next week I was due to go on the *Pop Idol* tour, which gave me the chance to do some serious thinking. The tour was amazing. We – the ten *Pop Idol* finalists – played twenty-three dates, taking in Sheffield, Birmingham, Manchester, Glasgow, Newcastle and London along the way. The first half of the show was pop, the second half was big band and we all had solo turns before coming together for the final song, 'My Way' by Frank Sinatra. The tickets sold out incredibly fast and the audiences were great. It was fantastic to be performing live again and, although it was a frantic schedule, we had a lot of fun on the tour bus that took us from gig to gig.

Meanwhile, I had to keep bluffing Simon Cowell and Pete Waterman. They both thought that I was signing to them, so it was a really tight balancing act.

Simon Cowell would call up and say, 'How's it all going?'

'Fine,' I'd say. 'I saw Waterman.'

Then Pete Waterman would call up. 'What's happening?'

'Er, I'm busy doing the tour.'

I think Pete Waterman must have known that something was wrong, because I hadn't contacted him for a couple of weeks. I had deliberated my dilemma while mulling over my feeling that in order to establish my own career I had to place myself as far away from *Pop Idol* as possible. I must see Simon Fuller. It was time to talk to the man to whom I was contracted and explain my situation. I had no other choice.

chapter eight

mercury rising

The icy water hits me. It drenches my head and drowns me in shock. I'm completely stunned, aware of only myself and the bite of the cold blast. I open my eyes and turn – Cyrus stands giggling, holding an empty bucket. The radio announcement echoes in my head: '"Colourblind" is the UK's official number one!'

I see Mum and Dad and Aria rushing towards me, arms outstretched. It is a special, surreal moment. We hug each other and shout and dance around the garden. If any of the neighbours are watching they must think we've gone mad.

'Number one!' we shout. Over and over. '"Colourblind" is number one!'

Simon Fuller agreed to see me as soon as I came back from the *Pop Idol* tour. Sitting on a black leather couch in his office, I opened the conversation by saying, 'I'm very grateful for everything that *Pop Idol* has given me. It's been an eye-opening experience and I can't thank you enough for the way you've treated me.'

'But I feel that my hands are tied behind my back,' I went on. 'All I want to do is sing the songs I write, and play my guitar. I feel it's time for me to go my own way. The direction that Simon Cowell sees for me is very different from the one I envisage. I don't think he knows exactly who I am, which is fair enough, because I've only just figured out what I am, or where my ambitions lie. I'd really like the freedom to do this on my own terms. I'm not happy as things stand. I want to leave.'

After blurting this out, I expected some antagonism from Simon Fuller. But he seemed to really comprehend my dilemma. I think he knew that I wasn't some marketing man's latest brand and could sense that I was my own entity. He was supportive as he talked through the pros and cons of my situation and came across as being amazingly calm. He spoke in such a gentle and eloquent manner that just being in his presence was soothing. Yet his reaction caught me off guard. I thought I was going in to stand my ground and so it knocked me off balance. I couldn't believe that he was so understanding.

I looked up to see a huge array of MTV and Brit awards lined up on a shelf. Seeing them reminded me of Simon Fuller's success, but his words came across as the words of a very understanding man, in complete contrast to the conversation I'd had with Simon Cowell in his flat. But then I remembered how reassured I had initially felt hearing Pete Waterman's words for the first time. I reminded myself to stay on course.

I persisted. 'I'm looking to be free of any contract that would prevent me from making my own music,' I said, heart in mouth.

'I understand,' said Simon softly, adding that he would speak to his lawyer. And so the meeting came to an abrupt end.

I couldn't believe it. Sitting on the couch, I felt light-headed as it dawned on me that the only thing that was holding me back from leaving the room was the sweat between my palms and the leather. There was nothing else. As I left,

'I'm looking to be free of any contract that would prevent me from making my own music,' I said, my heart in my mouth.

Simon said, 'If you want any guidance or advice on management, I'm here for you. I'll always try to give you impartial advice.'

While looking out the train window on my way home, my brain just went into autopilot, rushing through all kinds of possibilities. What happens now? What do I do? It was only later that I registered quite how generous Simon Fuller had been with me.

There was a part of me that felt guilty about turning down what Simon Cowell and Pete Waterman had to offer, especially when I thought about how much I had put Mum and Dad through. I must have pained and stressed them beyond belief. Through all my ups and downs they bled all the love, support and patience anyone could ever give. Just before the final *Popstars* audition, I told them not to worry about me, that I was excited about the

future. But instead the audition had set off a string of events that resulted in some very testing situations for them.

I think my parents were disappointed when I turned down the Xenex deal, although by now I had paid off the £12,000 debt with my fees from the presenting job and the G-A-Y gig. It wasn't because they were worried about supporting me financially. It was my wellbeing that they cared about. They just wanted to see me happy, making music. I remember my father telling me, 'I would sacrifice my future for your future. I'd do anything for you and your brothers.' When he said this I realised that as his son I had a responsibility. My responsibility was to be responsible for myself. And for every action there is a reaction. I promised myself I would never consciously make decisions that might result in stress for my parents.

All these thoughts were buzzing round my head as I sat waiting on the stuffy, stationary train; the driver wasn't the only one suffering from signal failure. It wasn't just that I wanted to make Mum and Dad proud. There's a big difference between wanting to please your parents and being frightened that something you do will pain them and cause a family problem or rift. But did that mean compromising my dream of writing music? Would my parents understand my decision not to sign with Simon Cowell or Pete Waterman? I hoped that they wouldn't be disappointed. I had to have faith that everything would work out for the best.

I knew I wanted to work with the best people in creative music. I wanted to learn from the top producers. Right up there was Steve Lillywhite, the legendary producer who had crafted several seminal records, working with great bands like U2 and Travis, to name but two. Pete Glenister had worked with Steve Lillywhite and Steve's ex-wife Kirsty McColl. So we sent a demo of 'Colourblind' to Steve's new London office at Mercury Records, not knowing that he had just been made a managing director of Mercury Records, under the Universal umbrella.

The timing of what happened next was unbelievable. Steve walked into his office after returning from America, only to find 'Colourblind' on top of a pile of CDs on his desk. After playing it, he phoned Pete. 'Who is this? Is this a band? I want to meet them!' he said. Because he had been living in America, he was unfamiliar with *Popstars*, *Pop Idol* and me. Later that day I found it hard to take in what Pete was saying when he told me that Steve Lillywhite wanted to meet me. I didn't sleep a wink that night.

Since I hadn't yet been officially released from my *Pop Idol* contract, my cloak-and-dagger meeting with Steve was very film noir. We met in a back-street Turkish restaurant off Kilburn High Road, a stone's throw from the Marriott Hotel. It poured down that night and I remember feeling wet, exhausted and extremely excited. Steve was a ball of energy, inspiring, highly animated, his hands moving all the time he spoke. He had rock-star hair, shot through with blond highlights, and sharp blue eyes that looked *into* you when when you spoke. I was thrilled just to shake his hand.

We had a conversation about my musical influences, and talked about the kind of album that I wanted to make. I explained that I wanted my music to be a fresh collection, from 'Mocking Bird' and 'Colourblind' onwards, because I felt that I'd been through a huge change. My debut album should reflect where I was in my life. Steve was on my wavelength and seemed to share my excitement.

Everything fitted. I learned that Mercury had once taken the lion's share of the UK market with global artists like Elton John, Texas, Bon Jovi and Shania Twain. But in recent years new domestic signings floundered and its market share declined. Hard times had called for harsh measures and Mercury dropped many domestic artists. Spurred by the success of new acts like Ashanti and Ja Rule the company was looking to make a fresh start – with two

new managing directors. Steve was seen as a pioneer producer who would revolutionise the company musically; Greg Castell was the marketing genius who had helped orchestrate many multi-platinum album campaigns – Enrique's *Escape* is among his triumphs. Together they would help turn around the company's fortunes. In many ways, Mercury's enthusiasm was like that of a brand new record company, but it was an established major label and it was hungry. It was as hungry as I was. It was perfect.

It was beyond belief. Six months previously I had written a song called 'Mercury Rising'. I knew it was a sign! Omens brushed aside lie as ashes, but if you see the significance in the ember of a coincidence, it can grow into a fire. The feeling in my gut was so strong. Nothing was going to hold me back from signing with Steve.

At the end of our conversation, Steve offered me a record deal. 'Darius, this feels good. I like your attitude, I love your music.' That was all I needed to hear. I was over the moon.

When I told Steve how close I am to my parents, he wanted to make sure that they were happy and fully informed of his record offer. And I still wanted their endorsement before I finally signed to Mercury. So Steve flew up to Glasgow to see them. That night I spoke to my father and asked him what had happened. Dad had asked Steve about his plans for me and he had said, 'I was looking for a true artist, and that's exactly what I've found. My plan is not to change Darius. I'll support and guide him, but let him grow of his own accord.' My father said to me, 'Darius, these are the words of a wise man. We support you fully in your decision.' I remember thinking that it meant the world to me that Mum and Dad had given me their blessing.

The next morning I got a voicemail from Simon Fuller. 'If you need management, the door's still open,' he said, reminding me that as well as helming commercial brands like *Pop Idol* and the Spice Girls he also managed songwriter artists like Annie Lennox.

Listening to the message, I remembered handing him a copy of the 'Colourblind' demo at our meeting. 'This is the song that I want to launch my career,' had been my parting words.

'The middle eight needs work, but it's great,' he told me on the message.

It meant the world to me that Mum and Dad had given me their blessing.

He was right – I ended up re-writing this part of the song. I couldn't help thinking, Wow, this man is *on* it!

I was struck by his insight. I had never met a businessman who had such a creative capacity. Since our last meeting I had realised that any uncertainty I might have had about Simon Fuller stemmed from my previous experiences. A feeling that he must be too good to be true also fuelled my caution. But this apprehension was erased by the way he handled the issue of my contract. He had been gracious, a gentleman – and had acted without business self-interest. He was *considerate*.

I remembered what Simon had told me about his business partnership with Nick Godwyn. I had already met Nick. He was the kind of man I knew I could grow to trust. Simon and Nick were exactly the sort of people I wanted to manage me because they understood me and now shared my creative ambition. I called Simon back. Brilliant 19 would be my new managers.

As soon as the rumour hit the grapevine that I was free of my *Pop Idol* contract, interest from other major labels sparked. It was ironic. There had been a time when they wouldn't return my calls, and now offers flooded in. But it didn't matter. I had my sights set on Mercury.

Everything flashed by after that. I made sure I hired the best lawyer to negotiate my contracts with Brilliant 19 and Mercury. It wasn't long before I agreed the terms of a five-album deal with one of the most powerful men in the business, Lucian Grainge, the chairman of Universal.

On the eve of my signing I had dinner with Nick, Steve Lillywhite and Greg Castell at Bluebird on the King's Road. Lucian had mentioned to Steve that he might drop by if he was in the area. While we were ordering dessert, an authoritative voice cut through, 'Death by chocolate, every time.' We looked up. Lucian had arrived. He sat down and we shared a dessert while I picked the brain of a superlative businessman. He was a family man, a football man, a man I respected greatly. It was no coincidence that he was in the area that night. The next day I signed. Then it was time to celebrate. Big time.

First I went to a champagne reception at the Mercury offices on the King's Road. It wasn't how I imagined a record

> *It wasn't long before I agreed the terms of a five-album deal with one of the most powerful men in the business*

I was finding it difficult to sleep at night because I was so excited. My mind would race, but not with stressful thoughts this time. It took me weeks to calm down. How lucky I am! I kept thinking.

company to look. It was more like a big house than an office, very simple and modern. The boardroom walls were covered with multi-platinum discs. I'm in good hands, I thought.

It was the first time I met everyone from the A&R, radio, television and promotions departments and it was quite overwhelming, a blur of hands and faces. I knew that I was going to be working very closely with this new family and I wanted to give each one of them individual attention. After all the trials and tribulations I'd been through, I had learned that success is very much about teamwork and relationships.

I was very excited. This was the beginning of something. I felt that we were all on the same team and, if I was the striker, I had some brilliant athletes behind me. I don't know if I conveyed all of this to everyone, but I think I got the message across to Steve and Greg. As we were photographed in front of the Universal sign with champagne glasses raised, I felt very happy.

I threw a party like there was no tomorrow. It was the kind of house party I used to go to when I was fifteen or sixteen, when someone would take over their parents' house and trash it, using the bed as a trampoline and literally swinging off lamp shades. It was a messy night and there was vomit in the kitchen sink the next morning. All my best friends were there. Johnnie flew down from Glasgow with Aria and together with Sean and Simon we had a riot. Instead of drinking for escapism that night, I drank in celebration. It was a completely different dynamic and a wonderful feeling.

I was finding it difficult to sleep at night because I was so excited. My mind would race, but not with stressful thoughts this time. It took me weeks to calm down. How lucky I am! I kept thinking. To have the endorsement of a major label investing millions in my career seemed incredible. It gave me a tremendous surge of creative energy. The flood of lyrics and melodies that had been welling up inside me came pouring out. It was like a river bursting its banks.

I'd been waiting for this feeling for so long. It was like when you're on holiday and you have that clinging sweaty feeling caused by the humidity of the air and sun on your body. You're dying to dive into a swimming pool or the sea. When you finally do jump in, the feeling of cool water on your skin hits you with such a force that you are completely overwhelmed.

Not long after signing to Mercury, I saw Pete Waterman and Simon Cowell at the *Heat* charity auction in aid of CRUSAID. They arrived together and the three of us were asked to pose for photos on a bed covered in silk cushions. Pete and Simon pretended to have a fight, with me in the middle, representing their very public argument over me on *Pop Idol*, I suppose. What no one else realised was that there had been a much more recent tussle. We were all very friendly and jolly, but there were definitely some undercurrents.

I shook Pete Waterman by the hand and said, 'Pete, I am so sorry that things didn't work out with us, but I had to do my own thing. I hope one day that you will understand that.' I felt that he brushed off my words and I was disappointed. I realised that by not signing with him, I had hurt the feelings of a man whom I respected greatly. Dad called my mobile phone that night, and I told him what had happened. 'I don't think that a successful man like Pete has ever come across someone like you, with such a strong conviction for writing music. You were prepared to take a risk and turn down a big offer. I don't think he understood the depth of your feelings. Don't worry, Darius.'

When I spoke to Simon Cowell I found that what I said harked back to the lyrics of 'Gun To My Head'. 'I just had to be what I could be,' I said. 'I hope there are no hard feelings.'

'No lovey, no darling. Good luck tonight!' he replied, then laughed and walked off. What a guy.

I had been asked to perform a song, but I wasn't sure what to sing. It wasn't the right situation to debut 'Colourblind', so I was thinking of performing 'More Than Words' by Extreme. Then I remembered that it had been covered by Westlife, one of Simon Cowell's acts.

I called my friend Pete Glenister. 'Will you come down and do a song with me?' I asked.

'Sure, what is it?'

'I don't know yet.'

'Are you joking?'

'No.'

Pete arrived as the dinner finished. 'Let's do "Faith" by George Michael,' I whispered to him a few moments before we were due on stage. I felt that the sentiment of the song was just right for the occasion. I sang it to Simon Cowell, but he just talked to Pete Waterman throughout the whole performance.

Ironically, I had been at the *Heat* CRUSAID auction exactly a year before and watched Hear'Say perform 'Pure and Simple'. Jonathan Ross was the master of ceremonies and at the end of the night he had asked me to sing 'Baby One More Time' one more time. I refused. 'Not even for charity?' he asked.

'No,' I said.

'Not even to raise £50 per table?'

Well, I couldn't turn down the chance to raise £10,000, so I got up and sang it a capella. I didn't enjoy the experience. I felt that I was essentially being pulled up on that stage as a spectacle. So it was great to be there a year later, performing in my own right. It was a real reminder of how far I had come in such a short time. I feel very lucky that these days I can use my profile to raise money for charity and work as an ambassador for the Prince's Trust.

If I wanted my music to stand apart from the hype of the programme, I would have to wait. I was willing to take the risk.

Initially, I had a panic about wanting to put 'Colourblind' out as quickly as possible, well aware that you could release 'Baa Baa Black Sheep' on the back of *Pop Idol* and it would probably have been a hit. It was, after all, the longest-running advert in the history of music, the most awesome marketing machine ever to be wielded by a major label. Even after the show had finished, there was still momentum to the hype. But if I wanted a shot at having a long-term career, not just an instant hit, I knew I must leave a six-month gap between *Pop Idol* and my first release. I asked Steve Lillywhite what he thought.

'You're right,' he said. He talked to Greg Castel and came back with a great plan. 'We'll release "Colourblind" in the summer on the basis of strong radio promotions.'

It was the opposite tack from Pete Waterman. If I wanted my music to stand on its own, without the dazzle of the programme, I would have to wait. I was willing to take the risk. I wanted the launch of my music to be about laying the foundations of a career. That meant visiting pretty much every radio station in the UK over the summer to promote the song in person, but I was prepared to work hard. I had to be.

At my first meeting with Steve Lillywhite I had said that I wanted my album to be a collection of new songs, without really thinking through exactly what that meant. It obviously made complete sense, but I soon came to realise that I'd set myself a huge task. I had six months to write and record my debut!

The next few months were spent living and breathing music. Most days I'd be in the studio until 2a.m. or 3a.m., then decide to sleep on the couch because I had to be back there in the morning anyway. Every day I woke up feeling excited.

I recorded the main body of the album with Pete Glenister and Deni Lew, but I needed to vary the production on the album so Steve suggested working with hot up-and-coming producers in Los Angeles. It was a buzz arriving at Heathrow and getting an upgrade to business class, then getting on the plane and being upgraded to first class. I'm lying in bed on a plane! I laughed to myself as I looked out at the clouds. And I'm going to America to write music. It was almost too much to take in.

I arrived in LA to blue skies, and met the Matrix producers at their studios just outside Beverley Hills. The Matrix are Graham Edwards, a gifted guitarist from my native Scotland, his talented, witty, inspiring wife Lauren Christy, and Scott Spock, a gentle giant and genius with all things technical. Individually they had different approaches to music; together they blended rock, pop and R&B. We hit it off from the start.

They played me some songs that they had written and produced for a young female solo artist, and I thought 'Complicated' and 'Sk8er Boy' stood out as being huge hits – and of course they would be, for Avril Lavigne. I wanted to do something with a rock element to it and we came up with 'Incredible'. It would become my third top-ten single.

Being in Los Angeles was just a great vibe for me. While I was there, I came across a cool basement art gallery downtown, which turned into an unlicensed club at night. I liked the fact that it was a bit of a shady place. You had to knock on the door and get the once-over before they let you in.

A couple of months later I went back to LA for a photo shoot. We drove from Los Angeles to Las Vegas, stopping at a little town called Barstow halfway between the two, where the photographer took a wide range of shots, including the photo that I chose for my album cover.

Back in the UK, before I did any TV appearances or radio roadshows, I had to put together a band. For the first time in my life, I was on the other side of the auditioning table. I must admit that I was nervous about whether I was going to find the right musicians. Were they going to click with the music? Or would I have to make do with people who, although great musicians, just needed the work and didn't particularly like the music? Sometimes that happens. I also wanted people I could get on with. We would be living in each other's pockets over the coming months, and perhaps beyond. This was not about doing a couple of TV appearances with these guys. It was about spending every waking hour together and long, claustrophobic journeys in a tour van.

The auditions were held at Terminal Studios, Tower Bridge. There were around a hundred musicians there and my musical director was slowly making his way through them when I arrived. 'Try to put together a list of the top five musicians and I'll see you in an hour,' I said to him on my way to the green room.

'Don't you want to hear them play?' he asked.

'No, it's more important to see how I get on with them.'

I'd been through the whole audition process and realised that the reality of a callback audition was fairly pointless. If you have a chemistry with someone, then that's the one to go for. There's no point in beating around the bush or hearing someone play a dozen different songs and looking at their CV. It should be a much more instinctive process.

I hit the green room and started introducing myself to people. I asked everyone about their ambitions and musical tastes. It was a very informal interviewing technique, a test of character and chemistry. I played 'Colourblind' and asked for an honest opinion. By this point I had begun to learn how to read people better. I also knew much more about the music business and the characters in it. I felt that I could tell when someone was being sincere or not, especially since I knew that people disliked me after *Popstars* because I had perhaps come across as being insincere at times.

I narrowed the group down to fifty within the first half hour and twenty within the next quarter of an hour. Within an hour I had a list of my favourite three. I chose them because I felt I could get on with them best; it was nothing to do with their musical skills.

'Who are your top five?' I asked my musical director, who presented me with his list of names. 'You're winding me up,'

If you have a chemistry with someone, then that's the one to go for.

I said in disbelief. Amazingly my top three were in his top five. It made sense. I probably liked them because I felt they had a similar work ethic and passion for music as I did.

Without a second thought I rang up Nick and told him who my preferred choices were for the band.

'Are you sure? You've only been an hour.'

'Positive,' I replied.

In late May 2002 I shot my first ever video, for 'Colourblind', in Spain. We stayed in a Moorish villa in the middle of nowhere, on the edge of the Sierra Nevada mountains. It was exhilarating. I was like a kid in a candy shop. There was a helicopter, Grand Canyon-esque scenery, a vintage Mercedes-Benz and, of course, a breathtakingly beautiful girl. I couldn't believe that the jobs of fifty people had been created as a result of a song I'd written.

Shooting the video was like a dream. It was a surreal experience that involved putting a machine in the middle of the desert to create rain as the sun set on the hard, cracked, desert terrain. It meant being flown by helicopter to the top of a canyon and walking to the very edge of a mountainous drop with my guitar slung over my shoulder, while a helicopter panned over me. It was unforgettable.

The shoot lasted three days and on the last night the crew threw a raucous party. The following morning I awoke just as dawn was breaking. I walked onto the balcony outside my room. The view took my breath away. The Sierra Nevada drops and cliff faces were stooped before me; to the left of me an elegant Moorish temple towered on top of a foothill, set against a stunning backdrop of snow-capped mountains. Far off in the distance I could see a picture-postcard village, whitewashed and staggered against the horizon. To my right rolled a vast expanse of cornfields. As the sun rose, it touched the tips of the corn heads, making them sparkle and with the wind's caress they were glittering like a golden ocean. I looked left again. The full moon looked down on the exquisite scenery. It was as if heaven had fallen from the sky.

The experience was almost too much for me. It was so beautiful that I just stood there and cried. Thank you, God, I am so lucky, I thought. I desperately wanted to share what I was seeing with my family. It was a glimpse of something greater than I could imagine. I didn't know if I fully deserved to experience it.

It was so beautiful that I just stood there and cried. Thank you, God. I am so lucky.

I didn't think I had much chance of getting to number one...

For all the hard work that I had put into my career, I was still at the very beginning. Although so many people were saying 'well done' to me, and in some ways signing a record deal had felt like crossing the finishing line, seeing this scene reminded me that I'd only just started the race. It was stunning and I'd love to go back there one day.

That summer my band and I hit the road and performed up and down the country, completing the roadshow circuit from Party in the Park to Feel the Noise Live and Summer Excess. It was a 7a.m. start seven days a week to cram television, radio, local press, travel time and all the gigs into a demanding schedule. My tour manager Johnny Brosnan, became a good friend. Johnny B had seen it all before, tour managing everyone from All Saints to Blue. He drove us 12,000 miles in five weeks, the average driver's annual mileage – not including the helicopter rides and plane journeys that he organised. I have never met a more efficient man in my life, and I learned all about stamina from watching him work. It was like being on a summer camp, a big adventure with the boys. I was happy to work long days, because when you do something you love, it doesn't feel like work.

We opened the show at Party in the Park in Hyde Park, London. It was amazing. 'Colourblind' had only just been released to radio and wasn't in stores yet, but when I ran from one side of the stage to the other I was greeted by the biggest Mexican wave I've ever seen. It was a defining moment for me. Looking out at the crowd of 100,000 people, I thought, I cannot believe I've been given the opportunity to do this.

'Colourblind' was released on 29 July. I decided to spend the weekend with my parents in Glasgow because I wanted to be with them when the new chart was announced on the Sunday evening. I didn't think I had much chance of getting to number one because Gareth had been riding high at the top of the charts with 'Anyone Of Us (Stupid Mistake)' and his sales were huge. So I was speechless when my manager Nick called me and told me that 'Colourblind' had reached the top of the charts, out-selling its nearest rival at least twice over. Then I screamed. I took some deep breaths and tried to calm myself down. I didn't want my family to find out until Foxy announced it on radio.

My parents and brothers went mad when Foxy finally said those unforgettable words: '"Colourblind" by Darius is the UK's new number one!'

They let us play to the end of the song because the crowd were really going. There was more cheering when I was asked to play it again. It made me tingle. *Nobody told me it feels so good.*

They screamed and shouted and whooped. Meanwhile I was totally drenched and freezing cold. I couldn't believe that I hadn't heard Cyrus creep up behind me. But it didn't stop me celebrating and by the time we'd finished hugging and dancing around the garden, we were all completely exhausted!

It was a childhood dream to appear on *Top Of The Pops*. I had watched so many great performances on it over the years, and I couldn't help thinking about my favourites as I made my way to the *Top Of The Pops* studios. 'Karma Chameleon' by Culture Club, Madonna's 'Holiday' and Wham singing 'Wake Me Up Before You Go Go'. I had also been entranced by the sight of Kylie bouncing around in a shoulder-fit top and big hoop earrings to 'I Should Be So Lucky'. I think I joined a nation of young boys at the time who dreamed that she might babysit for them one day!

No longer on a student budget, I was finally able to wear the clothes that I'd always wanted to wear. I decided on ripped-up denims and a designer shirt for my first *Top Of The Pops* appearance. Then the director asked me to start the song with my back to the audience. Well, that's a bit boring, I thought.

A few minutes later I walked past a guy painting in the hall. Suddenly, I had an idea. I had recently been referred to as an 'underdog' by a fan and liked it. I asked this painter if I could borrow his paintbrush, then lay my expensive shirt on the ground and scrawled 'underdog' on the back. I didn't think anyone would notice.

Performing 'Colourblind' on *Top Of The Pops* was a dream come true. And I was petrified. I think I sang the wrong lyric on the second verse.

Everyone cheered. As we performed the first run-through, there was a technical problem but they let us play to the end of the song because the crowd were really going. There was more cheering when I was asked to play it again. It made me tingle.

Nobody told me it feels so good.

'Colourblind' was no longer simply about the colours of the emotion that you go through when you're in a relationship. It reflect the colours of emotion that I'd experienced on my journey through the highs and lows. I remembered feeling black and blue, feeling jaded. Suddenly the lines *You're the light/ You're the light/When I close my eyes* took on a different meaning. After so much darkness, the light was so bright it was almost blinding. I was finally doing what I'd always dreamed of and people were supporting me. They thought I was an all right guy. Thinking about it gave me a sensory overload. I was blown away, even though I didn't know then that in the press the next day, people would see the slogan on my shirt and like it, or that eventually 'Colourblind' would go on to sell 350,000 copies and be one of the radio hits of the year.

Another high point was performing at the O2 music festival in Ireland in August. As I went on stage, the presenter announced that it was my birthday and a cake was brought on. Suddenly 100,000 people broke into 'Happy Birthday'. The noise was deafening. A tear crept to the corner of my eye but I wiped it away before anyone could see. It was the absolute flip-side of that disastrous gig at G-A-Y the previous year.

Fame had become far kinder to me by the time I released my album, *Dive In*, at the end of the year. I noticed it in small ways. Firstly, on my way to do an interview at a TV studio, I heard a tune I recognised. I turned round, trying to identify what it was, and saw a girl go to answer her mobile phone. It clicked. 'Colourblind' was her ring tone. As she answered, I looked at her and smiled. Then I walked through some swing doors and smiled to myself as I left the sound of an excited scream behind me.

I think people were genuinely surprised by my album. I was certainly surprised by the glowing reviews. One of my favourites appeared in the *Sunday Times*. It read:

Here's a turn-up. Not only is this *Popstars* also-ran's debut a comparative masterpiece when lined up beside the efforts from his rivals, Gareth and Will; it could also, with the right marketing, be a real contender for US success. At a time when the talk is yet again of Robbie Williams's chances of Stateside stardom – and, after *Escapology*'s mix of calculation and poor-little-rich-man's whining, this may require divine intervention – here comes plucky Mr Danesh to knock Robbie for six. Co-writing all of the radio-perfect tracks, Darius rarely puts a foot wrong…Highlights include 'Rushes', 'Girl in the Moon' and the title track. Who would have thought it? Not, you suspect, Simon Cowell.

At the other end of the critical spectrum was *Smash Hits*, with another of my favourite reviews:

> If Darius's distinctive brand of pop has you all hot under the collar and clamouring for guitar lessons, his debut album will certainly tickle your taste buds with 12 self-penned insights into Mr Danesh's mind. Whether it's the romantic 'Simple Like The Truth', the catchy 'What I Meant to Say' or the bittersweet 'Gotta Know Tonight', each track is distinctive, memorable and wholly original. There is something for everyone who is craving an alternative to cheesy substandard pop.

I couldn't have been more thrilled when *Dive In* went platinum. It was a dream come true. The success of 'Colourblind' had been amazing enough, but this was something else. I couldn't help feeling proud of myself, especially when I saw how proud my parents were.

Almost a year after *Pop Idol*, I found myself back at Fountain Studios in Wembley for 'Record of the Year'. I sat on the couch and formed part of the final-five line-up with Ronan Keating, Will, Gareth and Atomic Kitten. Will, Gareth and I couldn't help reminiscing about the times we recorded *Pop Idol* in the same studios.

Holly Valance, Enrique Inglesias, Shakira, Anastasia and Liberty X had all been nominated for 'Record of the Year', so it was a big deal to get this far. In the end Gareth topped with 'Unchained Melody', Will was second with 'Evergreen', Ronan came third with 'If Tomorrow Never Comes' and I came fourth with 'Colourblind', followed by Atomic Kitten with 'The Tide Is High'.

At one point I looked up and saw Simon Cowell talking to my manager Nick. He left before I had the chance to speak to him, so I gave him a call. 'Darius, my boy, how are you? I'm so sorry to have missed you,' he said. I wondered whether he had been avoiding me. We chit-chatted for a bit and then he said, 'So, what was it like losing again tonight?'

I laughed. 'I actually think it's an amazing privilege to have been voted into the top ten. And, as someone pointed out to me, Will's song was a Westlife cover, "The Tide Is High" is a Blondie cover, the Ronan Keating song was a cover of a Garth Brooks song that was also covered by Barry Manilow; and Gareth's song was a cover of a Robson and Jerome cover of the original Righteous Brothers' song.'

I paused and caught my breath. '"Colourblind" was the only *original* song in the top five. So actually I'm going out celebrating tonight,' I went on. 'What are you doing?'

In March 2003, a year after the *Pop Idol* tour, I supported Shakira on the Bercy stage in Paris. Shakira is one of my inspirations, so I was very ecstatic

when I got the call out of the blue. 'Do you want to support Shakira in concert?' asked Nick. I thought he was joking. And if he wasn't joking, did he think that he needed to ask? I didn't hesitate for a second. 'YES!' I wouldn't have missed it for the world. The audience were a blast – loud and enthusiastic about the set, even though they were hearing the songs for the first time. They jumped and cheered and tried to sing along to *Dive In* – it gave me goose bumps.

But despite having had three top-ten singles and achieved my dream of a platinum album, tackling the *Dive In* tour has probably been the most challenging and anticipated experience of all. I felt honoured to have the chance to be working with such great musicians. I felt honoured that Deni Lew and Pete Glenister, my producers, wanted to take time out of their hectic production schedule, at a time of high demand, so that they could join me on tour as my vocalist and musical director. (It wasn't until 'Colourblind' that I realised that when Nicky Graham described Deni as his partner, she was more than a business partner. In 2002 they were married. Again not everything was as it appeared.) I felt honoured that people wanted to see me perform. I got so excited about performing on my first proper tour I could barely contain myself when I heard that the first gig in Glasgow was sold out. I wanted to thank my fans for all their support and show them how appreciative I was.

As the tour rehearsals rolled on, I had time to look back at the amazing roller-coaster ride that has turned my life upside down. Sitting on my tour bus, sifting through old photos and scattered memories, I scribbled thoughts about the the first leg of the journey I am on. I've never kept a diary, but now I've written a book. I hope you've enjoyed it.

I've realised that I've got even less time to write my second album than I had for *Dive In*. I'm going to have to work harder than ever. I know that the coming year is a challenge, but I'm ready, gloves off, with a gleam in my eye.

I think I'm prepared. With my family and friends behind me, and the support of my fantastic fans, I know I'll be all right.

I think I needed to go through all the ups and downs that have lead me to this point. It helped me to appreciate what many people go through when they are humiliated, bullied or abused, whether in subtle or more obvious ways. I know I went through it all on a more public level, but I consider myself to be lucky all the same. I have had a very privileged upbringing, something I can never forget after hearing my father's stories about his childhood, war and revolution. Although I was bullied at school, I've had life easy. So I am truly grateful for what I've been through, because if I hadn't experienced it, I don't think I would have appreciated what I have now nearly as much.

I now know that happiness isn't about being in the press, getting good reviews or always being seen as a winner. It's about doing what you enjoy through the highs and lows, accepting what's on your plate and making the most of it.

I am standing on stage at the Glasgow Armadillo, waiting for the curtain to rise. Although I can't see them, I can hear the people in the crowd and feel their energy. Although my heart is racing, I know I'm always safe with my band. Pete and Deni whisper, 'Break a leg.' Nick gives me a thumbs-up off stage. I feel close to them all. My dear father and mother are out there. Aria and Cyrus are there. I can't wait.

The next chapter in my life is about to unfold and I have no idea what twist or turn awaits me. I've got a lot to do in a very short time. But right now I'm focused on that curtain in front of me. As it rises I get ready to sing 'Sliding Doors' to the cheering crowd. After all I've been through, it feels like I've waited a lifetime for the moment. 'Hello Glasgow! I'm home!' A roar erupts.

With my eyes closed it sounds like crashing waves on a dark, stormy night. But in my mind there is nothing but blue sky as I stand on my shore and look out at the horizon, blinded by the light. A vast ocean stretches before me, rippling into the distance. The waters are calm. And as I stand in awe of the deep blue unknown, I wonder if my heart might swell with gratitude. Will life always be this good? Do I really deserve all this? The noise of the crowd gets louder. There's no time to think. The music kicks in. It's time to go on. Time to dive in, sink or swim…

I know that the coming year is a challenge, but I'm ready... I think I'm prepared. With my family and friends behind me, and the support of my fantastic fans, I know I'll be all right.

'Tomorrow we will run faster,
stretch out our arms further...
And one fine morning –
So we beat on, boats against
the current, borne back
ceaselessly into the past...'

F. Scott Fitzgerald *The Great Gatsby*

acknowledgements

Swimming rather than sinking is achieved with the help of many people. owe my family more than I can express in words . Thank you Mum and Dad for your love, strength and wisdom ('I want *all* of them'). Bless you Aria and Cyrus for your inspiration and compassion. Aya-jan – I couldn't have done it without you. Cyroosh – thanks for the styling tips. Papa, I love you. You were right: never, never, never give up.

My eternal gratitude belongs to the special people in my life: Auntie Ashraf, thank you for guiding and healing me; Uncle Harold, I will always carry your stories and advice with me; my great friends Simon and Sean, our memories will be the Bedrock we build our future on – bring on the JDs and B&Js (from HK to LA)!; Johnnie, can you feel the love in this book?; Rachel, 'Would you like a drink of our wine?'; Ryan, where are the twins now?; Jon, embrace the weirdness; Jacqui, now look what you've done. To the incredible girls who've inspired my songs – I think about you every time I sing them. Love and a big hug to all my family and friends for their unswerving support and to the important people who let me do what do – the fans.

Thank you to my insightful manager Nick Godwyn of Brilliant 19 (you were right, 'it's all about Nick') and his fantastic assistant Kate Lower (I'd be lost without you); all the talented producers and writers I've had the privilege to work with especially my creative family – the wonderful Nicky Graham , Deni Lew (my 'Brown Girl in the Ring'), my long-lost big brother, Pete Glenister and of course the Matrix; the whole team at Mercury (bring on round two!), especially the legendary Steve Lillywhite, Greg 'Marketing Maestro' Castell and Lucian 'The Godfather' Grainge; my loyal tour manager Johnny Brosnan ('come on the drummer!'); my band and the entire crew from the *Dive In* tour; all the sexy people at 19 and of course the Pop Guru, Mr Simon Fuller. Respect and many thanks to the people who've helped me on my journey: Simon Cowell, Pete Waterman, Nigel Lythgoe, Nicki Chapman, Neil Fox, Ken Warwick, Claire Horton, Cam, Howler and the Thames gang, the generous John Simpson, the effervescent Tracy Chapman, John Webber, friends at CSS Stellar, Judd Lander, Paul Lennon, Andrew Thompson and the lovely Netia Hibbert.

I am indebted to the following people for their help in creating my first book: my editor Emma Tait (you have wings of patience); all my new friends at Headline; from 19 Merchandising Maya Maraj ('I ain't getting on no plane you crazy fool') and the eminently calming Joanna Reesby; the designer Dan Newman (thanks for letting me help); gifted photographer Bright Masih and the wicked team that worked on the shoot; and most especially to the intelligent and very sexy Rebecca Cripps for her words of wisdom.

Thank you to Taylor Fergusson and all the team, Gibson guitars, Hugo Boss, Levis, Ted Baker, Clinique, Top Shop, Orange and Shellys.

Oh, Mum and Dad – 'Finished!'

Credits

58: 'Chrysalis To Butterfly' (Danesh) © Copyright 2002 Universal Music Publishing Ltd. Used By Kind Permission Of Music Sales Ltd. All Rights Reserved International Copyright Secured.

93: 'Mocking Bird' (Danesh/Glenister/Lew/Graham) © Copyright 2002 Songs In Lew Ltd, Universal Music Publishing Ltd, Zomba Music Publishers. Used By Kind Permission Of Music Sales Ltd. All Rights Reserved International Copyright Secured.

121: 'TROUBLE' (Berryman/Buckland/Champion/Martin) courtesy of BMG

143: 'Gotta Know Tonight (Danesh/Frampton/Braide) © Copyright 2002 Universal Music Publishing Ltd. Used By Kind Permission Of Music Sales Ltd. All Rights Reserved International Copyright Secured.

150: 'Make It Easy On Yourself' (Bacharach/David) courtesy of Windswept Music London/Universal. Used By Kind Permission Of Music Sales Ltd. All Rights Reserved International Copyright Secured.

183: 'Colourblind' (Danesh/Glenister/Lew) © Copyright 2002 Songs In Lew Ltd, Universal Music Publishing Ltd, Zomba Music Publishers Ltd. Used By Kind Permission Of Music Sales Ltd. All Rights Reserved International Copyright Secured.

185: Reproduced by the kind permission of *Smash Hits* magazine.